Fr. Henry Hanses —

"How Handsome Before the Lord!"

a brief diary of a Kentucky mountian missioner

Prepared and edited by Rev. Ralph C. Hartman

Published by Katherine Landwehr

Printed in the United States by
St. Martin de Porres Lay Dominican Community

Send comments or questions to:

Rev. Ralph C. Hartman
c/o St. Henry Church
3813 Dixie Highway
Elsmere, KY 41018

Acknowledgement

With grateful appreciation to Katherine Landwehr — who funded this project; to Patricia Ober and Scott Eppley who computerized the text, and to all who contributed material. — Rev. Ralph Hartman

Table of Contents

Prologue	1
Foreword	11
Van Lear, KY — August 28, 1926 — The Diary Begins	15
Epilogue	147

Prologue

Ask anybody who knew Father Henry Hanses and you're likely to hear, "He was a saint!" The man was remarkable for solving people's problems in totally original ways. St. John's parish in Covington, Kentucky is filled with stories of how he met the challenge of each day with great faith, humor and a loving spirit.

Father Henry resolved to keep a diary when he was sent to the mountains early in his priesthood. For two years, he was faithful to the task. Then, unless lost manuscripts come to light, he continued a kind of diary only on the occasion of annual priests' retreats.

People delight in telling stories about Henry Hanses. Hundreds of people knew Father Henry as a genuine friend of the poor, one who showed respect, trust and compassion to all. [Editor]

Ray Schmitz was one of Father Henry's closest friends in his parish at St. John's The following is his capsule of the priest's life:

Mounted on the wall at the stairwell landing of my home is a picture of the Right Reverend Monsignor Henry Hanses. By such a title, one would know that this person was a priest of the Roman Catholic Church. However, the title was much too formal for the many who knew him and developed a sincere affection for him. To all, he was known simply as Father Henry.

Father Henry's photo-portrait has been placed on the stairwell wall for a purpose. As I retire to my bedroom every night and pass by his picture, Father Henry's image is a reminder that he was not only a very dear friend, but one of the finest human beings I ever had the privilege to know.

Henry Hanses was born in Detroit, Michigan on October 28, 1896. After the death of his father, he went with his mother to live with his uncle, who was a priest, Monsignor Anthony Goebel.

Spending most of his childhood and youthful years living in a church rectory, it seemed inevitable that the young Henry Hanses would follow in the footsteps of his uncle. And on June 19, 1919, he was ordained into the priesthood.

Father Henry spent most of the early years of his vocation in the mountain region of Eastern Kentucky, around the area of Harlan County. He returned to Northern Kentucky in 1948 to become assistant to his aging uncle, Monsignor Goebel at St. John's Church in Covington, Kentucky. After Monsignor Goebel's death in 1954, he was appointed pastor of St. John's Church.

Having been a member of St. John's parish since 1951, I was involved in some of the activities of the parish. Since Father Henry encouraged such efforts on the part of the laity, he and I developed a deep and lasting friendship. I had casually known him for some time and had heard many stories of his generosity and love for his fellow-man. It was not until I became more closely associated with him that I began to fully realize the very humane qualities which he possessed. He was truly a "man of the cloth", totally devoted to his religious vocation, especially in his charitable works. Anyone in need could come to his door and would not be turned away empty-handed.

With the passage of time, Father Henry gained assurance that he could share matters of confidentiality with me. He would discuss with me various requests for assistance which were mostly financial in nature. I was amazed at the amounts of money which he had "loaned". I was also amazed at the amounts of money never repaid. However, he never seemed a bit concerned about any non-repayment of money. In many instances, I honestly believe he did not expect any return. It was the belief that he had helped someone in need which brought him a sense a joy and happiness.

While Father Henry's charity and generosity gained him a reputation of love and respect, he was also a man of extreme patience. There were many instances when demands were placed upon him for his time by individuals who literally spent hours explaining every detail of every "problem" in their lives. Many would seek him out routinely and repeat the same details. Father would listen attentively and always provide words of encouragement which might help them cope with the demands of life. I cannot recall any instance when he was ill-tempered.

Father Henry also possessed a very deep love for children. He had learned some magic tricks with coins and playing cards. He was also a good storyteller, particularly ghost stories. He loved occasions when there would be a small group of pre-teen age children that he might entertain. He would begin with his feats of magic and then would tell one of his ghost stories, always ending with a very dramatic climax, bringing screams and howls from his young listeners. To anyone observing, it was difficult to determine who enjoyed the event more, the children or Father Henry.

In October, 1971, Father Henry suffered a severe stroke. Although he partially recovered, he was left with a permanent speech impairment. This severely hampered his priestly duties. He retired from active service and spent the balance of his life in a convalescent home. This was very difficult for him. His lack of ability to converse and the isolation of his surroundings were burdensome to him. As one who had given a lifetime of involvement to the everyday events of society, he must have had some very lonely hours. I visited him regularly and, as always, he was always cheerful, never uttering a word of complaint.

In January, 1982, Father Henry passed away. The funeral service at his beloved St. John's Church where he had served most of his priestly life was attended by an overflow throng of religious and laity. They came to pay homage to a man who touched their lives by his humility, by his patience, by his charity, by his concern for his fellow-man, by his acceptance of whatever it might be that life had prepared for him.

Father Henry Hanses was not only a dear friend but the most compassionate human being I ever knew. In my lifetime, he was truly a "man for all seasons". (Ray Schmitz)

St. John Parish Bulletin Reflected Hanses Humor

A yellowing parish bulletin dated May 9, 1971 has a short piece called:

"One of Those Days": Monday, May 3rd

This is a true account of one day in the life of the pastors of St. John's:

7:20 —Gave out a lunch ticket

9:00 —Gave a lady $25 for some oral surgery. Checked later. Appointment not kept.

9:15 —Grocery order to a lady with an infant on her arm.

9:30 —Grocery order to a lady with a two-year old by the hand.

10:00 —Another Grocery order.

12:30 —Lunch ticket.

1:00 —Took a sick lady to the doctor.

3:00 —Unloaded a truck-load of furniture into the rectory basement. Family dispossessed.

5:30 —Three telephone calls while at supper table.

6:00 —Church window broken.

Next morning this note was found on the altar in church:

"Mr. Priest: My name is............ We live at ....
My girl friend's father took $65 from her and told us to get out.
We have no food, no money for rent......"

Another Written "Keeper"

Father Henry had a great knack with words and, more than most of us, would use the printed word to give power and permanence to his thoughts. His Christmas cards were often personalized in touching ways. An old Barton-Cotton nativity card carried the following message:

On Christmas Day, I remain alone with my thoughts.
On Christmas, I let nothing disturb me.
On Christmas, I travel back over that long, long trail of the past and I tarry at each loved spot where a friend crossed my path.
On Christmas, I live in the past.
I feel again, on Christmas Day, the glow of your friendship.

His greeting to friends in 1953 contained a unique little folder with the following:

A Christmas Story
By a Fourth-grade Boy.

Act I: Bethlehem

JOSEPH: ZZZZZZZ ZZZZZZZ ZZZZZZZ

MARY: ZZZZZZZ ZZZZZZZ ZZZZZZZ

JESUS: ZZZZZZZ ZZZZZZZ

Act II: Bethlehem

ANGEL: Wakest thou, Joseph, you got to takest the Child and His Mother and flee-est into Egypt.

JOSEPH: Wakest thou, Mary, we got to takest the Child and flee-est into Egypt.

MARY: Wake up, Jesus.

Act III: On the way to Egypt

JOSEPH: Silent

MARY: Silent

JESUS: Silent

Act IV: Egypt

JOSEPH: Look, Mary, those people are worshipping idols. Isn't that awful?

MARY: Look, Jesus, those people are worshipping idols.

(Jesus looks.)

THE IDOLS: Crash! Boom! Bang!

(The End)

More Recollections

Howard Nienaber recalled the following story, typical of the wisdom of Henry Hanses:

As a young man starting out in the landscaping business, I worked for several churches. Among these was St. John's Church in Covington, where Father Henry Hanses was pastor. One day, after finishing the job as contracted, I went into the rectory to present the bill to Father Henry. As we talked, he somehow sensed that I wanted to give a discount to St. John's but was hesitating because I could not afford to give the same discount to the other churches where I was working. He came up with the solution immediately. He said, "Charge a fair standard price for your work at St. John's. Do your charity work for your home parish of St. Henry's in Erlanger. When you become rich, you can extend your charity to other churches". That sound advice stayed with me throughout my years of service.

Robert Brady's wife, Jeanette, recalled how Father Hanses made them a loan in a real financial crisis. This was in the midst of blessing their marriage, baptizing their children and receiving Bob into the Church. The young family was paying back the loan, a little each month, when Father Henry called to say the debt was paid in full — a gift to their new-born son.

John Hoffman recalled how his mother died in 1962 and his father tried to drown his sorrow in drink. He finally took his father to see Father Henry one evening "and he never ever drank again — a miracle!"

Jim Scanlan remembered the Spring of 1933 when he was in the Civilian Conservation Corps and his company had established a tent camp on the side of Pine Mountain in Harlan County, Kentucky. Father Hanses came to the camp and offered to say an outdoor Mass. After several Sundays, he invited us to attend Mass at his church in Lynch. This was a great event, we arrived in several trucks and were treated royally by Father Hanses and his parishioners.

Recollections of Monsignor John Murphy:

I first recall Father Henry when I was sent to Villa Madonna College in September, 1949. He was on the faculty and staff and taught a course in Fundamental Religion which was really catechism for students who had been in public high school. He was also director of student activities. Everyone loved him. He was always upbeat and friendly. One funny story that has been often told relates how he helped the students create a lunchroom in Bernard Hall's second floor on Scott Street. On the day it opened, Henry had managed to go to the funeral home and get a number of floral arrangements which he brought in, tagged with cards that read "Congratulations from Harry Truman!" and "God bless you! Pope Pius XII"

Henry arranged an annual outing at the home of relatives in Franklin, Ohio. He loved getting the priests from Villa Madonna College to go there for dinner and cards.

He was a humble man, he was not a scholar and wasn't one for in-depth debates or discussions, but he was always ready with a one-liner or a sentence of homespun wisdom. He delighted in telling stories on himself. I remember his laughing as he told about giving a ride to a hitch-hiker and then allowing him to sleep in his car in the garage after he got home. The next morning, his car was gone!

As an example of his humility, I was impressed as a young priest when, once, after going to him to confession, he asked me to hear his and he got down on his knees.

His generosity was so widely known that people lined up to get help, but they also lined up to give him things as well! I went to him once when someone had asked to borrow about $2000 which I didn't have. It was a former student who was then a family man in real need of a lift. Henry quickly gave me the money for him and, later, when I was worried that it hadn't yet been paid back, he told me not to worry and that when it was paid back, I should keep it and lend it to someone else who might need it.

He helped a fellow priest who was having trouble. He would run up big bills at the religious goods store and then be unable to pay. Henry paid the bills and the priest gave him several pieces of religious art he had bought, some of which he gave to me when I admired them. One had to be careful about that, because if you liked something, he would give it to you!

Katherine Landwehr came to Henry for everything. In those days, she did a lot of traveling and would bring him very nice art pieces. As soon as he figured he could give them away without

Katherine Landwehr, an active realtor at 85, made the Hanses Diary Project her consuming passion for years, so well and so long did she know him and admire him.

Early photos of Henry (Smiling wasn't allowed back then.) Here are Henry's mother and sister, Uncle Father Goebel, and brother Father Al Hanses.

Young Father Hanses.

her knowing it, he would do so! I think she also may have bankrolled some of his giving practices.

Henry was a clean desk man. He seldom had more than a book or tablet on his desk. He really lived a simple life style. I know of nothing to which he was actually attached. He helped out whoever was in need. (John Murphy)

Editor's Comment

It would be fascinating to find letters and diary entries from Henry's older brother, Father Alfred Hanses. The two of them corresponded a great deal. Some of Henry's diary seems to imply that the reader knows the rest of the story since Al was the one who received Henry's entries and, we presume, Henry received Al's. Two brothers could not have been further apart in their approach to life and ministry. The photograph below shows the Confirmation class from Henry's first year at Lynch, Kentucky, following Father Al's pastorate. The picture tells it all. Whereas Al held back many children from being Confirmed because they had not learned their catechism to his satisfaction, Henry held back no one and quickly got caught up by inviting all the children his brother had refused. Apparently, presiding Bishop Francis Howard approved.

This picture shows the Harlan County Confirmation class at Lynch, KY. It was so huge because Father Henry's brother Al Hanses, previous pastor, was much more demanding of the children before allowing them to be confirmed. Henry took all the "rejects" his first year.

Foreword

I knew Henry Hanses by observing him at clergy gatherings, infrequent visits in the 60's when I was a young priest working in the marriage office of the diocese, and especially through the stories brother priests would tell about him. Some admired his accounting method that began with a given sum in the bank and ended with the year at another given amount. Between these two, Henry placed the proposition that he surely was not a thief and therefore, one way or the other, everything had to balance. And it always did.

Henry himself told me of being in the shower once, lathered from head to foot, when someone began ringing the rectory doorbell with such an unforgiving passion and relentless disregard that he grabbed a towel and bolted for the door to so shock the visitor that she fled at the sight of this fairly upset "Soapman"!

Bill Huston, a Black orderly at Carmel Manor Nursing Home where Henry spent his last days, is the author of the touching memoir which follows:

REV. MSGR. HENRY A. HANSES
1972 — 1982 CARMEL MANOR

Father Hanses came into our lives in the latter part of 1972. He came to visit Father Leo Streck, who was at the time, Chaplain of Carmel Manor Nursing Home. Father Streck became ill and retired to "Regina Cleri", the priests' wing. Father Hanses took it upon himself to see that Father Streck got to Jewish Hospital three and four times a week, in his Plymouth, for treatments. He would go in the ambulance with him when he became quite helpless. He was blessed with a private duty nurse and a loving brother, in the person of Father Hanses, who stayed with him 15 to 16 hours a day, rubbing his feet, scratching his head, giving him milkshakes, and doing whatever he could to put him at ease.

Father Hanses helped whom, and where, he could. He brought Father Lubrecht to see Father Streck every Wednesday for two years. God called Father Streck home on November 3, 1975.

Father Hanses retired to "Regina Cleri" on October 5, 1975. Oh what a great loss to St. John's Church in Covington where he served for 30 years. But what a blessing for Carmel Manor. Father Hanses found a very dear friend there, Father Poole, who was 11 years his senior. He would take Father Poole for walks, drives, and sit on the porch overlooking the Ohio River, enjoying a cigar and a little drink. Father Hanses spent many long hours with Father Poole.

Father Hanses continued his chauffeuring by taking Father Lubrecht to and from the doctor once a week in 1978 and 1979. He taxied Father Gockel to wherever he had to go. Quite often he taxied Sister Rose Bernadette to the dentist, doctor or wherever. He took no money for gas nor did he ever stop for gas. Sister thought that was the only Plymouth that ran off of air and water. She asked Father Hanses if his gas multiplied like the loaves and the fishes. He said, "Maybe." Father Hanses, being a lover of mankind, touched the lives of many people, with his big smile and a nod of peace to everyone.

Father Henry and the Plymouth that "never needed gas" as he transported all manner of ailing priests and laity to their doctors and hospitals.

He brought donations of food to Carmel Manor's Bazaar for five years. He had St. John's Choir singing during the holidays for the residents. His many acts of charity proved his being a Man of God.

Every day of the four seasons, he would walk in the woods. He liked the snow and the grass on his bare feet. He was another St. Francis of Assisi. He loved birds. They would peck on the glass of the dining room, looking for Father Hanses, while the Fathers were having their breakfast. There were sparrows, robins, blue jays, chickadees, titmice, yellow hammers, woodpeckers, and he was the only Monsignor who had a *cardinal* that did not give him orders.

There were some raccoons that he wanted to come up on the porch. He would soak bread in rum to introduce himself. He would say: "Come, come," and they came, out of love for him, and the rum.

Father Hanses had many young priests visit him. This was not usual for the priests' house. One day, I was delivering mail to the priests. I knocked on his door and there was no answer, so I walked in. There was a young priest kneeling on the floor going to confession. This was the answer to all these young priests visiting. Father Hanses was like the Cure of Ars. I always thought he was different from the others. He was a very special priest. He radiated Christ. It was peaceful to be in his presence.

For about three years, every Tuesday, Father Hanses spent time in the priest's chapel with the tabernacle door opened. We had soft spiritual music, prayer, and meditation. Employees who were off duty and lay people from the outside would come. They said it was so peaceful and they felt the presence of Jesus. They looked forward to coming back.

Two months before his last Christmas, he put money gifts aside for people who assisted him. "Maybe," he thought, he wouldn't be here for Christmas.

On January 19, 1982, God knew he was tired from long hard work, and that it was time for him to come home and rest, and also let him know that his work, well done, was finished.

A year after his death, I went to St. John's Cemetery to visit his grave. He was buried next to his uncle and his brother who were both priests. This was in January. Father Hanses' grave had green grass on it. The other two had no grass.

(Fond recollections of one who knew him.)

Editor's Comment

One of my intentions in putting this material into book form is to please Miss Katherine Landwehr, today an 85 year old former hardware business woman and still active Realtor. Katherine was a dinner guest of Henry's on more Saturday evenings at St. John's church in Covington, Ky., than anyone can recall. Her conviction is that Father Hanses will be an inspiration to bishops, priests and laity alike. She especially believes that even this very partial biography will give young men a vision of priesthood that will help reverse the sorry prediction of a near priestless Catholic Church in America. Even from my limited view, I agree with Katherine upon whom I have bestowed the title "Lady" for her lifelong service to the Church and its clergy in the Covington diocese.

I also hope this little book will inspire other friends of Father Hanses to take the time to write down their recollections of this modern St. Francis. If a life so well lived counts for anything, he is a citizen of Heaven, a saint in the opinion of all who knew him. Eventually, we might have a fair biography of the man, the priest, the lover of the poor that Henry Hanses was. I hope someone will call me to say they have "the rest of the story" — the comparable diary and history of Father Henry's priestly brother, Alfred, the recipient of Henry's diary entries.

I want to acknowledge the kindness of everyone who sent me photos or clippings or personal recollections about Henry. Charlie Deters, whose wife Mary Sue was an example of how Henry somehow provided for children from the mountains of Kentucky, to find their way to an education and many opportunities beyond the grim life style of Kentucky coal towns. Sister Theresa Wolking, O.S.B. who was the provider of many insights into Henry's fatherly regard for the Sisters of St. Benedict at St. Walburg Convent overlooking the Ohio in Kenton County. I must be sure to return to the convent archives the fascinating 34 page little leather bound book that delightfully recalls Henry's hiking friends of his youth. They came from many local families especially the Fedders who gave a Sister and two priests to the church, both of whom became bishops of the Maryknoll missionaries, giving their lives for the people of Peru and China. Of course, Msgr. Ralph Beiting, Henry's successor has many stories to add about the Appalachian area of the diocese of Covington.

Father Hanses makes diary entries assuming that the only person to ever read them is his brother, Fr. Alfred Hanses. This must be the reason he so casually drops words and phrases that would not be familiar to a general audience. Most are Latin church terms or perhaps local idioms.

The Diary Begins

Van Lear, Kentucky — August 28, 1926
Saturday — 6:40 p.m.

Perhaps this diary idea will begin once more a chain of correspondence between you and me that was mighty pleasant from five to fifteen years ago. What a story these pages will foretell! I would not read them now if I were given the power to do so. How merciful God is that he does not show us the bitter struggles ahead! There! I'm already guilty of breaking one of my resolutions. I am going to make it a point to always look for a humorous side to a difficult situation. It's not necessary to make of this an exact chronology — as you suggest, write as the spirit prompts. So, at this time, I will record nothing of Himlerville, other than the fact that I was there last Sunday. (I'll make provision next time to get a pen that does not flow so freely.) Not since September 1908 did I feel a transition so keenly as I did this one last Monday. That September in 1908 was my first at St. Charles. About the fifth day at St. Charles, it dawned on me that I was expected to study; the five o'clock study stunned me. It is (was) new to me that school was not "out" after the last class! And I had to do this every day for 106 days, I was told! Oh how tight my throat became! That's the way I felt Monday. But I didn't want to run away; I didn't wish for anything different; fate was not cruel; this was the place for me to work out my soul's salvation. I wanted you and Elizabeth and even uncle, and still I didn't exactly want you, but I felt so much closer to you and to all my friends. I never asked myself whether I liked my appointment or not. Life is but a preparation for death (Mercier in American Mercury) and the thought uppermost in my mind was and is, as I said before, to work out my soul's salvation and to do that I would rather not choose the field of my labor. Father Dyer, I believe, contributed more than anyone else to the information of whatever priestliness is in me. And so, I turned first to the altar, for a priest's zeal is indicated by cleanliness around the altar, said Fr. Dyer. The Blessed Sacrament was practically never kept in the tabernacle and, when it was, an electric light kept vigil before it. Fr. Whalen had just supplied a new altar. I turned to what takes the place of a vestment case and my zeal flamed up and said — a vestment case must be procured. I opened a drawer and a feeble mouse crawled out and dropped to the floor. I laughed — poor as a church mouse — I never understood that as well as I do now. The only thing the poor fellow had to eat was a stale newspaper,

And so, each day I have tinkered around a little, not in a hurry about anything, but concerned principally at working out from the altar. Just so, Fr. Dyer taught us to be priests from the inside out, not from the outside in, that is: be priests at the heart first, preach by being good.

My what a pleasant evening! I'm blue, I'm lonesome yes, but I would not have it otherwise; I must get used to it.

About the rosary — I have not missed a day since December 8, 1923, not three years yet. But it's a habit now that I hope I will never lose. My rule has been to let it be the last thing of the day, even if the "day" went beyond midnight. And I often say it in bed. The point is — I want it to be the very last thing on my mind. I'll try to keep it close to ten o'clock. My Sunday prayers, including my rosary, always are for father and mother, brother and sister; the ten o'clock rosary will daily have a special significance.

Speaking of hobbies — I want to read and have begun a history of the church. I plan to read an hour a day; I want to make that a rule: not less than an hour. But I dream of something else, too, and am almost afraid to mention it for fear that it's only a passing idea. Why not take up music? I have decided to wait perhaps a year before settling the matter.

I'll begin to finish for today, not because you finished on the sixth page but because I just got in from our meeting at Jenkins and want to get a few things ready for my first trip back to Covington tomorrow. It took me five hours to get to Jenkins and eight and a half to get back. If you leave Jenkins at 3:00 a.m., you can make it to Van Lear in about five hours,

I received word from Covington today that Fr. Streck was in St. Elizabeth's Hospital having sustained a broken arm and a broken finger, as well as a lacerated hand in an automobile wreck!

I have no envelopes suitable for these leaflets here, so I will mail this from Covington.

Van Lear — Sunday, September 13, 1926 — 8:10 a.m.

First, I wish to make a correction — I had intended to mail my diary from Covington, but before leaving for Covington, I found an envelope large enough to carry my diary to Lynch.

I did not think that you meant a daily chronicle when you suggested that we begin a diary. For ten years I have been keeping a diary but sometimes months elapsed without a word of record. I cannot make it a daily affair very well because of my traveling, though I would have written at Himlerville if I had thought of bringing my diary along.

I'm just beginning to feel at home on my mission; I'm just beginning to get into the work. Up until now, I have done very little except unpack and travel to Covington. In writing what is to come, I am fully aware of the fact that in a few years, I may retract much or all of it. I don't presume to know all about something of which I know nothing nor do I presume that I am better qualified for this mission than someone else, though I might be. Moreover, in these pages I am going to be honest; I am going to record my impressions and my conclusions as I see them, just as you do yours. Nor will I ever attempt to preach to you between the lines — I'm going to give you a picture of my life.

I've decided to make my headquarters at Van Lear. Fr. Whalen wanted to move them to Ashland, seventy miles from here. It never will be a home; it's no more than a boarding house. I will be away most of the time and for that reason cannot ask any lady that suits me to come here from Covington and be far more alone than Veronica is in Lynch. But this is just the kind of headquarters I want; I want solitude and there's the first point of difference between you and me. I have already felt a desire, when away, to get back to Van Lear and solitude. Duty, of course, calls me away regularly; in fact, I want it so I would not want continual solitude. I just want to get to it, then after two or three days, I am ready for action again. So solitude is one reason why I decided to make Van Lear my headquarters. The principal reason is because it is central.

I have not much order to my day. I get up about 6:30 and am ready for Mass by 7:00. After Mass, there is straightening up to do till breakfast at 9:30. Up till now it's more straightening up till I get tired and then I take a walk to the post office which takes forty minutes for the round trip. Then more work around my room and answering of letters till I'm tired again and then I make an hour's adoration, which rests me in

Father Hanses, the circuit rider, with the "best horse in the country!" 1922

my body and mind. In fact, I go to church with the thought that I am going to rest. After that, I may read a while but, so far, I have had little time to read, but that will come. After supper, in the dark, I like to walk around a bit in the yard listening to the voice of God in the stillness, then saying my rosary, and then go to bed and dream day-dreams till I fall asleep. So far, I have been very tired every evening and can easily sleep sound for nine hours and more.

I can see plenty of work ahead. The church and house here at Van Lear need attention; four or five places have not yet been visited; a lady in Martin Hospital, whom Fr. Whalen anointed, is still living and I must go to see her. And I want to get to Lynch. But I would like to keep my trip to Lynch in reserve a while; I would like to keep it for a week when there is nothing on my mind. This we can talk over, when you come tomorrow.

And now it's almost 9:00 o'clock, I have already made an hour's adoration and, being Sunday, it was for you and Elizabeth and mother and dad. I now want to get the vestments ready for Mass, think over what little I will have to say in the way of preaching, meet the seventy or so men, women and children, perhaps hear one or two confessions and, after Mass, to have a little talk with the seven or eight children who probably will be present. I plan to tell the people this morning to live in God's presence; to say to themselves as they walk down the track or while loading coal, etc.: There is a God; He sees me and He loves me.

Himlerville — Friday, September 17, 1926 — 3:00 p.m.

This is my third trip to Himlerville and will probably be my longest stay in this town so far. This time I fortified myself with writing and reading material. Up until now, my extra moments were taken up by sitting around at Schusters or Noonans.

Though the month has seemed long, the weeks are short enough. Time is not going to drag. In fact, I see enough ahead for more than a month to keep my life from becoming monotonous. This morning I left you at Kermit at 9:50 and walked home over the company's private bridge and was in my room at 10:40 after a very leisurely walk. I then wrote two letters, put my room in order, brought a couple of pieces of candy to Ed and Jim Schuster, bought some thumbtacks and went to the church where I made an hour's adoration before I left. Then I had a little talk with the school children just coming out of school and it seemed to me that all the children must have been Catholic. After I'm through with this diary, I'll say some more office till suppertime at Noonans.

At 7:15 I have a date with Mr. Kolos for my first real lesson in Hungarian. I'm going to bed early tonight, last night having been the poorest I have so far had on the missions.

(A challenge to the engraver!) Life in Himlerville and Lynch was a study of the Depression.

The hot summer is past. The beginning of my working year looms ahead. Before time begins to drag, I will have seen Caspar, Ligon, Prestonsburg, Martin, Pikeville, Weeksbury, Estill, and even Elkhorn City in Fr. McCrystal's territory. On my next trip to Himlerville, I expect to visit Williamson, W. Va., and Stone, Ky. I wish also to show myself in Ashland which I may defer till my next visit to Covington. And all this time I intend to keep pushing the repair work at Van Lear.

"What will I do next?" is my motto and I have been asking myself that with regard to Himlerville. And I answer: continue your getting-acquainted work. The hardest birds to reach are the beau brummels and they will be the last ones that I will get to and the ones I am most desirous to get to. I plan to be a man's man and hope eventually to have many more men going to Communion regularly than now but by men, I mean first boys and after that anything I can get with pants on. The thought uppermost in my mind is — save the families with many children to the church. The present generation of children will not work at Himlerville when they are mature, at least the majority will not, for the simple reason that there will be no room for all of them. The families here are very prolific. So my desire is to implant in these young hearts so great a love for Mother Church that they will later on successfully ward off the onslaughts of indifferentism. We have here about 200 school children out of 100 families. Lynch has 1500 children out of 2000 families is my guess. On second thought, I suppose 1500 families would be closer to it, wouldn't it?

September 18, 1926 — 3:45 p.m.

As I went up to the church at 7:30 for Mass, I met Miss Monarch, a Catholic public school teacher, waiting for Mass. I expect to do considerable business with this lady, who is rather backward but who likes to teach in Himlerville because she likes the children. I heard three adult confessions before Mass and was deeply edified by the number of those who attended Mass. There are many cures for the blues, as well as for discouragement, at Himlerville. After Mass, till 12:30, with the aid of three girls — though there were two too many — I worked at a general housecleaning, burned up a young carload of trash and put order in the sacristies. Then I went to my room and studied some more Hungarian. At 3:00 I took my second lesson in Hungarian and after that strolled down to the church where, to my surprise, I found five girls and three boys waiting for me to come and hear their confessions. I'll hear again this evening.

Tomorrow at 8:00, the aforementioned children have promised to go to Holy Communion. I plan to pray with them. In the afternoon, Mr. Kolos will take me to three or four families that I may make their acquaintance. I plan to visit at least three, and not more than four, families every Sunday when I can find the men at home until I have met every Catholic in town. If I visit too many, I will become confused.

And so I'm beginning gradually to take in the situation; a system is beginning to function. So it is also outside of Himlerville; as my plan matures, I will record it: 1st, 3rd, and 5th Sundays at Himlerville, 2nd and 4th at Van Lear, 2nd also at Paintsville, and the Tuesday after 1st at Louisa — though I'm going there this Tuesday also. Wednesday I go to Weeksbury — whether it will get a regular visitation remains to be seen.

Van Lear — September 21, 1926 — 12:20 p.m.

I left Himlerville yesterday evening but not until after I walked over three miles through the mines, under the worst of conditions, I was told, that could exist in a coal mine. I picked up a Monday's Enquirer on my way to the train and to my dismay, learned that my favorites were trimmed 13 — 1 — I refer to the Goldenrods. I looked a little closer and saw that they had a home run, a three-bagger, two doubles, eleven singles, five walks and five errors favoring them and their opponents had only six hits. So I wired from Kermit, W. Va. to Covington and at Louisa got the answer: "Enquirer wrong. Goldenrod's win 13 to 1." It read like a racing record.

This morning at Louisa, everybody overslept. I was called at 6:18, said Mass, ate my breakfast and was ready for the 7:00 o'clock train at 6:59. At Van Lear, something had actually been done: the new stove was up, the plumbing in the bathroom tended to and four-fifths of the church ceiling painted. Then I got to my mail which calls for half a dozen answers today because tomorrow and Thursday I spend at Weeksbury and Wayland.

I read your last diary account while waiting to purchase a box of shoe polish. You state that you will be in Jenkins Monday; I'll have to wait till Tuesday. If the carpenter had begun his work this week, everything would have been finished before Sunday; the plumber is finished, the painter is at work, but the carpenter and electrician have not shown up and now that the work is started, I want to stick to it till it's finished. When I leave for Jenkins, I won't see Van Lear again until I'm through with Himlerville. So I want to be here at the beginning of next week. In case I get the carpenter going this week yet, I could keep my appointment, but I don't want to wait till the last minute.

I have sent for the geological survey map of this district and if I get it in time, I plan to walk from Himlerville to Van Lear, which is not more than twenty-five miles. The return from Himlerville by railroad necessitates a night in Louisa, whereas by walking, I can leisurely make it in eight hours.

Incidentally, I will get an intimate acquaintance with real Kentucky life. I have yet to meet a non-Catholic with an Irish name! I may also learn that the road is fordable at certain seasons. Trains now run from Himlerville to Inez — eight miles — and the road beyond Inez is supposed to be a graded road.

My mail brought me news of Elizabeth's sickness — rheumatism the doctor says. The letter came from Sister Marcella, Joe's sister. I also received word of the death of Ralph Tuemler, the janitor and bank messenger at Peoples Bank. He leaves four or five children.

The painter just informed me that he was running short of blue paint and he has but five feet more to go. So he's going to paint the whole thing over in gray!

Van Lear — September 24, 1926 — 8:30 a.m.

Returned yesterday after a two days' jaunt to Weeksbury, which lies at the other extremity of Floyd county. It is about 53 miles from here and he who travels thither must change trains three times: first at the Junction catching the Big Sandy Special, the main train going south, then transferring to the Wayland territory and finally branching off to Weeksbury, this last train running off its course twice and nicely backing back exactly twice also.

Weeksbury cannot be "made" in a day unless one leaves on the same train he arrived on fifteen minutes after arrival. An eighteen year old lass took me to her mother's home. I used to wonder how the ladies hereabouts succeeded so well in keeping up to snuff about style, yet Sears-Roebuck can take care of that. But where do the local barbers learn their trade? I've seen every style of haircut in the Van Lear district that Covington can boast. Well, Dorothea Watsell took me to her mother and I was surprised when I saw the home. The clothes and the haircut did not prepare me for the lowly hut that was this girl's home: twelve inch boards covered, for the most part, with tar paper.

The welcome was genuine: Mrs. Watsell is a 300 pounder and usually such peoples' hearts are as big as they are. Mrs. Watsell is the mother of fourteen children, ten of whom are living, six at home. The two boys 10 & 22 are good clean fellows, thoroughly Americanized in ways and speech. Their name is German; the parents are 3/4 Slavish. I ate heartily at supper though the cooking was to me unappetizing. I ate several things that night and next day, such as fried oatmeal sausage, that I thought were going to make me suffer. But I experienced no bad after effects. Even the coffee, which I had to drink in a hurry, didn't bother me. After supper, we talked a while and then I went to bed. I had a very good bed. About a half an hour after the light was out, I heard a creeping and a scratching under my bed that I could in no way explain. It wasn't mice, nor rats, nor snakes. Then another noise and the room was soon saturated with "poison gas;" one of the cats had gotten into my room and began to suffer from "pressure on the brain," ran around a bit and then furtively tried to make a hole in the floor. I got up and opened the door and tried to chase the dam thing out, but it ran everywhere but through the door. I left the door open, turned out the light and kept my nose close to the pillow. Though the door was open, the intruder repeated his operation at least once more.

Next morning I did not say Mass. About nine o'clock, Mrs. Craynor, one of the Watsells, came for me in a Ford and took me to the church, a beautiful little church on a little hill, all alone. The KKK greeted us from the cross. Until recently the white robes marched about twice a week through the town. A window on the farther side had been broken (and since repaired) and all the electric globes stolen and the vestments scattered through the church. The altar, vestment case, and pews are everything that could be desired. So I decided then and there, if ten people would come to church, I'd have Mass in the church; the last four or five Masses were said in Watsell's home. Mrs. Craynor volunteered to clean up the church and then we visited the Catholics of the town: first we visited the Menofskys. Mrs. was sitting up; they just brought her from Martin Hospital where she had been lying for about ten weeks as a result of an automobile turning a "somersault" — I have no dictionary yet! Five in that family promised to come to Mass whenever I would have it. Mrs. Spargo, married at Prestonsburg, promised also to come. I did not know of the nature of the marriage until later. The Mirofak children promised to deliver my message to their parents, one of whom was divorced and married a second time. One other family, whom we could not locate, is at present attending the Presbyterian church, the only other one in town. And that's all.

I promised them the fifth Sunday of the month; otherwise, the six men would not come. If the men respond and I find similar conditions at Wayland, and I expect to, the only solution I see is for the Bishop to put two of us at Van Lear, like at Corbin. But I better wait a few months before deciding such things definitely. At Van Lear, the painter will be finished with the interior before Sunday. The carpenter and electrician have not yet begun. I'll try my luck at them again today. Now for some breakfast!

Van Lear — Sunday, September 26, 1926 — 4:30 p.m.

Sunday afternoons in Augusta were spent with Elizabeth, Mary Bufner and Catherine Cook. At the seminary, Sunday morning was spent, often, in the penitentiary; the afternoons with one's particular friends. Little studying was done even on Sunday nights. At St. John's, every other Sunday afternoon was spent in opening collection envelopes. The alternate Sundays were taken up with visiting sick; occasionally I went to a ball game, Five o'clock generally found me headed toward the cemetery. Sunday evening found me studying one year philosophy; after that, mathematics.

My Sundays on the missions, so far, have found me visiting the parishioners. It's an awkward pastime but is aiding me to know my parishioners in a hurry. I visited four families this afternoon; one adult member of these four families was at Mass this morning. Almost everyone thinks I'm coming for money.

Yesterday and the day before were terribly lonesome days and I believe it was due to the fact that, because of the painting going on in the church, I did not reserve the Blessed Sacrament in the tabernacle. I made two hours of adoration today and, for the first time since several weeks before the Eucharistic Congress, am I "caught up." As soon as my next Emmanuel, one organ of the Eucharistic League, comes, I'll have you enrolled. I don't usually feel much attracted to make an hour of adoration; I have made it a matter of will power; and after I'm through, I'm grateful. Though I am "caught up," I plan to make an hour every day that I am not traveling. I hope eventually to have a plan for my whole day. At present that plan calls for a meditation in the morning, a holy hour, a study hour, an hour of spiritual reading and an hour of other reading, a walk to the post office, and a call on some parishioner. So far I never once have had time to get my whole schedule in, principally because of my heavy correspondence, which I hope soon to get down to one letter a day. One day I wrote twenty-nine letters, when writing to all the men who gathered together the $600 purse for me at St. Johns. I have, however, written as many as ten and twelve letters a day in answering accumulated mail.

By mailing this tomorrow morning, it will go out on the same train that I will be on Tuesday morning. I'll go south, this will go north, and we'll see how much longer it takes this diary to get to Lynch than myself. The carpenter has promised to come tomorrow; so has the electrician. I expect my riding trousers tomorrow (the bill has already come) and if my maps come too, I'll be all set to walk from Himlerville to Van Lear on October 4th. I am having high shoes sent from Sears-Roebuck direct to Himlerville. I decided on the high shoes rather than putts, so as to be able to walk through water deeper than the height of ordinary shoe tops.

Van Lear — October 5, 1926 — 7:15 p.m.

I had no leaflets with me at Himlerville or I would have sent some diary from there.

After you left, Fr. McCrystal and I sat around till supper and then came the show. At 4:00 a.m. next morning, my train left for Shelby and Pikeville; then I taxied to Williamson, where the door to the priesthouse opened itself for me as I mounted the stairs. Fr. Gleason knew I was Fr. Hanses and wanted to know why in thunder I stayed away so long. His housekeeper is a Covingtonian and knew me, I having prepared a cousin of hers for death about six months ago. I said Mass, breakfasted and chatted and at 11:40 left for Kermit and Himlerville. Saturday morning I had a long conference with Miss Monarch, the only Catholic teacher in the town this year. And this is our plan: two classes of catechism every Saturday afternoon at 3:00 o'clock — Miss Monarch in charge of one and I and Mrs. Noonan, a former school teacher, the other; Mrs. Noonan to conduct the class on the Saturdays that I am not there. Then on Sunday afternoon at 2:30, I'll have all the children for another instruction.

Sunday evening, Joe Schuster and I went up to see Mr. Himler. The doctor (the new one), the superintendent, postmaster and bookkeeper were there ahead of us. We chatted pleasantly till 11:00. Before we left, Mr. Himler bet Schuster a suit of clothes that he could reduce more in four weeks than he, Schuster, could.

Monday I visited a dozen families. In the evening I walked to Kermit and had less than a minute to spare to get my train. On the train I picked up a paper and read that the Goldenrods won the first game of a series of three to determine the semi-pro championship of Northern Kentucky. The night I spent at Louisa. At 10:00 this morning I said Mass here at Van Lear and practically ever since, I have been sitting at a table covered with mail.

October 7 — 6:45 a.m.

A little more work was done around the place. I now have a serviceable vestment case at a cost of $4.75; the electrician did his work and the painter finished his. The carpenter had more work to do: bookcase, coal shed, fence, etc., but died on the job. I don't know when the next man will come.

Yesterday I took the kit to Paintsville for Sunday when I expect to drive a horse so that I can get Mass in at Paintsville and here. There I found two sick people: Clarence Schmidt with a sprained ankle, ala football, and Mr. Singer down with rheumatism. I also met a Mr. Slager, one of the millionaire members of the oil firm, though there was nothing about him to indicate that he was a millionaire except the way he handed me a twenty dollar bill "for a couple of Masses for my father and mother and the rest for yourself."

The three of us, Mr. Schmidt, Mr. Slager and myself discussed the possibility of a church in Paintsville with the result that Mr. Schmidt will look around immediately for suitable property. Paintsville and Louisa would be a nice combination for another priest who could occasionally work in my territory also. I believe that some missions to non-Catholics in that territory by a trained missionary would be productive of good results. I walked home from Paintsville in a little more than an hour and a half.

Today I'm going to Wayland, about fifty miles down the river. My train leaves the junction at 9:08; instead of taking the 7:20 from here, I'm going to walk to the junction.

Next week I'm going to Covington but I may not be able to see the bishop because I saw in the Telegraph that he is booked for Lexington on the 12th. In case I can't see him next week, I'll run in the following week also and then have a day or two with you.

I have been asked whether "it would be too inconvenient for me to hear the confessions of the Sisters at Ashland, Ky." I have also been appointed school inspector for Ashland.

I was sorry to note in your diary that you have been melancholy again. I am saved from a similar fate, I suppose, because of my varied occupations. I have enrolled you in the Priests' Eucharistic League and I hope that will give you some encouragement. When I find myself getting blue, I pray the *"Oblatio sui"* that can be found among the prayers for Thanksgiving after Mass at the end of the Breviary. I also make this my morning prayer.

Van Lear — Saturday, October 9, 1926 — 8:40 a.m.

Whenever I land in a new town, I'm always a little anxious about the kind of welcome I'm in for. At Wayland, I found conditions entirely different than I had been used to: the only Catholics belonged to the "higher-ups." The manager, dentist, school teacher and a store keeper make up the Catholic population, I am told. The welcome I received was royal. My train pulled in before a turn-table at 12:15, I registered in a neat little hotel and had dinner. From dinner to 2:30, the time of departure, I was with one or more of the Catholics. I will say Mass there November 1, coming from Weeksbury on the other spur of the fork on October 31. I will say Mass in the dentist's office.

The two Schellinger girls, the school teacher and store keeper, hailed from Benham nine years ago and spent seven and ten years respectively at Corbin, where they became Catholics, and are steadfast in their faith though their father is a Protestant and their mother a fallen-away Catholic.

I don't believe that there are no more Catholics in Wayland, the prettiest town in my territory. There are foreigners galore and I'm going to find some

Catholics who have been chased under cover by the Ku Klux, who greeted everyone of Fr. Whalen's visits with a fiery cross!

Estill, Ky. is about four miles from Wayland and has four Catholic families, according to Fr. Whalen's record. I'll look these people up on November 1 and 2.

What must this country have been fifteen years ago, before the railroad came and before the oil wells and coal fields were operated!

Yesterday I finished cleaning up the church. It's just where I want it for the present at least. Now that it's painted inside, I can keep it clean. The next thing I want — maybe six months from now — are pews. Half of the excellent pews at Weeksbury may just suit me here.

Today I put in a $46 order to Sears-Roebuck — blankets, shoes, shirt and pajamas for the winter, also a feather bed for Mary. I find electric light lamps very cheap at Sears-Roebuck.

My mail is beginning to let up a little and I am glad. This week's mail, which includes last weeks because of my absence, brought me sixty-two Mass intentions. I'm way over a hundred now. Can you take care of twenty? I'm enclosing uncle's check for that amount, from whom the Masses came and who said nothing about the intentions. I conclude he wants them said *"secundum intentionem."*

Today I expect to do some reading; I have done very little reading in Van Lear so far. Tomorrow I will binate, first Mass at Paintsville, second Mass here. In the afternoon I hope to obtain the necessary signatures to the preliminaries of two revalidations — the ground is already prepared. The one, Pete Patrick (!), is the gentleman who stepped inside the church to watch us work where we were applying the vitrophane. And tomorrow night I head for Ashland and then Covington. I've been away for four weeks, which is quite a surprise around here, Fr. Whalen being known to have gone to Covington 4 times in 5 weeks.

Van Lear — Wednesday, October 19, 1926 - 11:00 a.m.

I don't feel like writing in my diary. Just got back yesterday after a nine-day absence, my mail has been read, and now it remains to answer it. For sake of record though, I must write the following: I like Himlerville more every time I go there; I would prefer to make my residence there, each one of my stays is becoming longer. The big drawback at Van Lear is the freedom of the house that Mary takes unto herself, especially in disturbing me in my study. I'd rather lead a hermit's life, like in my room at Oros's from which, however, I saunter when there's something to do and I can find work in Himlerville.

Sunday night the Catholics of Himlerville had a dance; there were four times as many people at the dance as the church can hold. It was a "grape dance:" the young folks and old danced under a frame from which were suspended large bunches of grapes, Anyone caught stealing grapes was fined by the judge, as much as the judge wished to fine him. It was the jolliest social affair I ever witnessed.

Tuesday morning, I said Mass at 6:00 am. and had breakfast at 7:00, At 7:20, Himlerville time, 6:20 Van Lear time, I started for Van Lear on foot. On the other side of Inez (8 miles from Himlerville), I lost my way, never to find it again. I followed a new graded road, which for a long time followed the course of the old one. I thought it would follow the same general direction as the old road and paid no more attention to my map until, at the end of a long, long gradual slope, the grading abruptly ended in a hillside. I found another road and, with the sun as my guide, with an occasional welcome from the C & O somewhere in the distance, I kept on. I walked for an hour and saw neither man nor beast, though once I heard a cowbell. After a long walk, I heard a rolling wagon below me and at a crossroad waited for a human being. I was told that I was four miles out of my way. So I walked some more. From then on, about 1:30 slow time, my course was down creek beds and up others and over two ridges by trail, It was amusing to be directed; everything went by creeks. I went to the head of Greasy Creek and then over a hill and followed the entire course of Pigeonroost Creek, over another hill and then down Millers Creek to Van Lear.

Noonan had figured the distance at 26 miles; I figured it at 22; I think I walked about 35. My left shank began to give out about 4:00 o'clock. I tried to spare it by making my right leg do more of the work in climbing and jumping. In the morning, I rested five minutes every hour; in the late afternoon, I was going slower and had to rest about every twenty minutes. I was afraid of becoming muscle-bound.

I got home at 5:45 slow time, having been 11 hours and twenty-five minutes on the way. When I began to eat, the back of my tongue hurts so bad I had to quit for a while; and my stomach refused potatoes and bacon and chicken but wanted peaches. There were no lemons in the house.

I left the table and said Vespers and Compline and then went back. I ate more peaches, some potatoes, two raw eggs and two cups of milk. I went to bed at 7:00. At 10:30 I woke up, both legs painfully tired; I took a good drink of whiskey and ate some candy and slept until 6:30 when I felt, to my very great surprise, stiff only in the left knee, though both shanks were a little tight. I ate a hearty breakfast, though my tongue and throat were still sore, perhaps swollen.

Never again!! It takes a geologist to find his way. Though some day, I expect to try this route: train to White House, walk ten miles to Inez, taxi eight to Himlerville, But not just now!

I was told when in Covington that the Corbin initiation had been postponed till October 24! I hope it's all over now and settled.

The bishop told me that I ought to attend the Conference at Lexington. You will probably want to continue in Covington because you go up so rarely, at least you did before May. In that case, I'll take the train for Covington the same night of the Conference.

I had intended to put down my impressions of interior Kentucky, but after an interruption, forgot to take up where I left off. The old log cabin is still very much in evidence and I had no idea that sorghum was produced in so great an abundance. At least at six different places were they making molasses out in the open, the old mule winding round and round, working a press, it looked like.

Van Lear — Sunday, October 24, 1926 — 5:30 p.m.

Recently I was appointed confessor to the Sisters of Ashland. So Friday, I hied myself thither. Fr. Bocklage keeps open house for all priests, at all times, whether they like him or not, and Fr., Cusack don't like him. After lunch, I did some shopping while Fr. B. took a nap, having arrived from Louisville at 1:00 a.m. We talked mountains a-plenty after supper and — races. If Fr. B. has any faults, I'd say he is too good a sport, He has a splendid library, especially of history and access to any of his books was given me.

At 8:00, I heard the Sisters' confessions, eleven of them, retired late and rose at 5:15 to take the 5:45 train to say Mass at Van Lear at 10:00. One of the Knepfles, road contractor of Newport, whom we met at Paintsville, boarded the train at Louisa, where the brothers landed another good job. They are finished at Paintsville.

Dook-a-la-dook! It's raining and Mary's cow didn't come home yet. Mary says she's going to tie her cow up on Sundays after this because she always comes home late on the Lord's day. She's been calling the darn thing for half an hour. She just now came in: "You booger, what's amatter mit you huh?"

Quite an event in the annals of Van Lear took place today: a taxi discharged a passenger before the church at 9:45 this morning. As the passenger entered the church, I went down the aisle to meet him and invited him to take dinner with me. He accepted the invitation. Even with Mr. McGraw, for such was his name, in church, our seminary collection amounted to only $8.03.

Mr. McGraw, P, J. McGraw, was fire marshal at a mine six miles from Fairmount, W. Va. in 1907 when a gas explosion in that mine killed 367 of the 368 men in it. The sole survivor was killed last week. I remember the shock. I was in the back yard in Augusta when mother and uncle excitedly ran out and wanted to know what made the house shake. The paper later said that the shaking was due to the W. Va. explosion. Up until this time, the safety department of the Consolidation Coal Company was under the mine management; now it's vice versa. And Mr. McGraw was sent here by the "Consulting Engineer;" as soon as he entered Mine 153, he ordered a certain section closed at once, much to the consternation of the management. He found 6% gas in this end and explosions have occurred in 5 1/2% gas pockets, Following this, Mr. McGraw was ordered to inspect all the mines thoroughly and, in his conversation with me, accuses the management of neglect. Please do not quote Mr. McGraw. He gave me a whole lot of inside information which I promised never to use against the company.

We talked until 3:00 o'clock and then went down to the recreation building for a soda; afterwards I went with him to the Club House, which is very attractive, especially inside. It was my first visit in the building. He then showed me a fan, explained its simple operation, and remarked that as far as he knew, none of the fans at Van Lear have been stopped once in fifteen years.

About that dog — it was never indicated to me in the slightest that there was to be a price on him. It now seems to me that he offered the dog to me in a moment of generosity and then regretted it. I hope the dog will become worth many times $35 to you, Mon. Frank.

October 25, 1926 — 7:50 a.m. — Monday

I was interrupted last night by the visit of Mr. & Mrs. Campigatto. They brought four quarts of beer and a bottle of apple brandy with them. Mary showed a bigger capacity than any of *them*; I limited myself to one shot of each: beer and brandy.

Mrs., Frank Burkard, address Monte Casino, Covington, has a book on raising and training police dogs. I am sure she would lend it to you. I would write myself and get one but I'll be on the road for more than three weeks beginning Wednesday or Thursday, and if you want it, you can get it quicker yourself.

For the sake of chronicle, I go back to Mr. McGraw. *He says*: A lady left Bp. Donahue several million dollars; of these Bp. Swint, his successor, spent a million and a half on missionary work, building churches and houses and buying property all over. A priest-friend of Mr. McGraw said the bishop was done spending money and has given up all hope of accomplishing anything permanent, especially among the miners.

I had planned to go into Magoffin County today but changed my mind because yesterday my left knee suddenly weakened after a three mile walk, the effect of my Himlerville-Van Lear walk,

Either Wednesday or Thursday I am going to Wayland; the next day to Estill; then by horse to Ligon, train to Wheelwright on the same day; that night Weeksbury for Sunday. Monday morning, All Saints' Day, I plan to leave Weeksbury at 4:00 a.m. and will get to Louisa at 10:00 for Mass there; then by bus to Ashland, stopping long enough to hear the Sisters' confessions, Tuesday morning, if I can't make it Monday night, I'll leave for Covington. Thursday afternoon, I may hear confessions for Fr., Bocklage for First Friday, though this is not settled yet; then Himlerville; from there to Lexington for the conference; back to Covington for a day or two; Ashland; Van Lear; then to Louisa where I have arranged through Castners for Joe Kuechle and Herman Schuler to join a hunting party. I myself plan to do no hunting. When they are through in Lawrence County, I am going to ask them to try to get through, with me, over Paintsville and Salyersville, to Mt. Sterling, the trip taking us through Morgan County, which is in my territory but where not a single Catholic resides that I know of. Beyond this, I have not planned, except that I am going to prolong my Himlerville visits and am going to start first Communion instructions in Van Lear for four little ones, whom I am going to instruct here in the residence,

I am half through with the Life of Bishop John B, M. David, coadjutor to the first bishop of Bardstown. I am enjoying it.

Van Lear — Wednesday, October 27, 1926 — 5:20 p.m.

I went to Royalton, Ky. today. aboard the B. S. & K. R. (Big Sandy and Kentucky River—which does not get near the Kentucky River) at Dawkins, less than a mile from Van Lear Junction. This particular R.R. has one locomotive of its own, which doesn't run any more, and it rents four from the C & O at $5.00 per day each. I learned today how to take the jerks at the end of a long freight; the baggage car was a boxcar on which the Ohio of Chesapeake & Ohio was painted Oiho. When the conductor came through, I showed him my pass; I must have impressed him with my importance because he became very obliging. I learned afterwards that this road does not honor C & O passes.

I sure saw life in the raw — mail was thrown off on this side, then on that, hauled away in the type of wagon that must have been used a hundred years ago. There was not a depot along the line. Kentucky, I knew, boasted a London and a Paris, but today I passed through Denver. At Royalton, there was a depot, housing the principal office of the B.S. & K.R. R.R. A thousand people live at Royalton, which is named after the Royal Bank of Canada, the railroad being a Canadian enterprise. Five miles further up the hollow is the only church of any kind in this territory.

At Royalton, I inquired for C.N. Polley, who had written to Van Lear about time of services. He is an unmarried man, 32 years old, lent to the R.R. by the C & O to straighten out some tangle. Fr. Gill from Richmond told him about the church at Van Lear. He knows Frs. Nott and Kilgalen well.

I was not prepared to witness the operation of the largest saw mill that I ever saw in my life. I saw 11,000,000 feet of lumber, drying and waiting to be shipped. I watched machinery handle tree trunks like I would handle an ordinary board. Royalton is in Magoffin County, not far from Breathitt. Bloody Breathitt County and Royalton, until a few years ago, were tough: the lumberjack hung his revolver on the same nail that held his hat, during working hours. There is not a foreigner in this territory and very few who are not native Kentuckians. Some other time I have been promised a ride on the logging train, that goes twenty-five miles into the woods.

I was introduced to about twenty people. I talked with Mr. Evans, the president of the R.R. for an hour. He was educated at Holy Trinity School in Ashland. He told us stories of these parts and vouches for their truth. A doctor in those parts has two remedies: pills and plasters. If it's a lady that is sick, he gives her pink pills; if a man, he gets brown pills. The Stumbo brothers operate Martin Ky. Hospital. The older, Walter, offered Mr. Evans one-third of all the fees he would collect from any accident cases he, Mr. Evans, might send to him and added: "I can be the best witness in the State in case you need me." Their hospital (at Martin) burned down twice. Now they can't get insurance. After their last fire, while the appraiser was on the scene, Walter suggested to his brother, Ed, to set fire to a piece of their property that was not producing revenue, but Ed objected on the ground that the time was not opportune. To which Walter answered that it would be a damn shame to make the appraiser make an extra trip. On another occasion, the two doctors were riding a railroad motor car on the main line, which the railroad had forbidden them. They ran into a crew of laborers and fractured the skull of one of them. The railroad was sued for $25,000 and judgment was pronounced against it, but the Court of Appeals reversed the decision on the grounds that the doctors were trespassers. The doctors were then sued; they claimed the man died of heart failure; the body was dug up to see where the skull had been fractured, but the head had been cut off! The doctors won. And so on.

I left after 2:00 p.m. About a mile from Dawkins, I got off the train and walked and beat the train to the depot. Tomorrow I go to Wayland and won't get back till November 14.

I remember the letter you wrote to me at Rome on the eve of your twenty-first birthday. I am writing these lines on the eve of my thirties. I was hoping the world would forget my birthday. No one around here, of course, knows about it. But like last year, I have received a bunch of effeminate greetings. Last year, everything came from women except your greeting and I hope you send me greetings again this year! Mary has volunteered to bring my mail to the Junction next Monday when I will pass through on my way to Louisa where I will say Mass. But I did not intend to write so much about my birthday as about your coming anniversary. And I, your junior, like respectfully to call your attention to this: on Judgment Day, you will be asked not how much you accomplished, but how much you tried or wanted to accomplish. I think that you have much to be thankful for as you look back over the last ten years. I am enclosing a holy card that would make a nice bookmark in the breviaries I hope you received. The breviaries are from Elizabeth and myself (and Joe with Elizabeth) and if, for some reason, they do not suit your taste, I know that you can exchange them for anything at Pustets.

I read with much pleasure that section of your diary in which you made a "confession." I, too, now say the prayers for before and after Mass; a thing I rarely did in Covington. Another item I have added to my order of the day is this: I read a chapter from St. Paul every day that I am in Van Lear in English and the same thing in German and I hope to add Latin and even Hungarian. And I memorize one sentence, in English, of that chapter for the day. My time has not yet hung heavily upon me, as you can well see for yourself from my diary.

I did not yet see Ben Hur. The next time you go to Covington, you must see Abie's Irish Rose, if you have not seen it. I have not seen it either and would be glad to see it with you. It has had a steady run in New York for five years and still going.

How's Rex?

Best regards to Veronica.

Not a line wasted!

Wayland Hotel, Wayland, Ky; — Friday, October 29, 1926 — 9:30 a.m.

Perhaps it would be better not to record my impressions until they would be more mature, but I am impatient to get to recording. My hand is tired after carrying a heavy Mass Kit for about a mile, but I shall write slowly. I have nothing to do till 5:30 tomorrow morning.

I arrived at Wayland at 12:15 yesterday noon and was welcomed by Mrs. Bohannon, the manager, as usual. Mrs. Bohannon, who now makes her residence in Louisville, is here on a visit and she welcomed me as if I were her own. She has a doctor, a dentist and an attorney for sons. I first took dinner; then chatted. At 2:30, took the train for Estill, perhaps a little over a mile away. The man I wanted to see boarded the train that I had just left. I engaged a Ku Kluxer in conversation. He was rather bitter, though he was Irish. Another fellow I spoke to was half Irish and half Indian. I located three Catholic families in Estill; a fourth was not at home and I heard of a fifth one. I wanted to say Mass here Saturday, but the people did not want it then so I said I'd be back at 5:30 in the morning and asked them kindly to round up the men. At 5:30 this morning, I was told that no men would be there, though one coolly told me it made no difference when he left for work. I sat around till 7:45, waiting for the children. At that time I began Mass, with three women and nine children, including one infant, present.

One family, Bukovich, whose oldest child is six years old, plans to move to Detroit for the children's religion sake; another, oldest child 13, plans to move to Elizabeth, N.J. for the same reason; the third, which has been in Estill longer than any other family and is there less than five years, will also move when the children become of school age. One of the women has promised to undertake the instruction of two of one of the other women's children; I will send her a catechism and prayer book. Fr. Poole teaches catechism by means of a Correspondence Course. I am going to examine his system.

I felt the necessity of a priest coming down here occasionally and saying Mass so as to impress upon the children the fact that they are Catholic. (These same children attend Sunday School.) But I also felt that the Holy Ghost will have to do most of the work. Catholic life is dying here; I have even heard of stories to the effect that the Ku Klux have driven Catholics away from certain places. All through the Beaver Creek section — Wayland, Estill, Garret, Martin, Ligon, Wheelwright, Weeksbury, the KKK is said to be entrenched. I can't say it is better that Catholics leave; I would rather see them hold their ground, But somewhere I'd like to see a Catholic school to attract Catholic miners with children to that territory.

Tomorrow morning at 5:30, I will say Mass here in the dentist's office. Six people are expected to attend. Here's their story:

Mr. Bohannon, manager. His stay at Wayland will now soon come to an end. The doctor has ordered him out of the mine because of high blood pressure.

Mrs. Bohannon, who is here on a visit.

Dr. Harry Bohannon, son of the aforementioned and dentist. He recognizes that he has made a mistake in establishing a business in Wayland. He belongs in Louisville, where his brother, the physician, could send him patients. The dentist is married to a non-Catholic to whom he did not introduce me last night; I hope it was an oversight.

Aileen Schellinger, a graduate of Corbin, and a business school in Cincinnati. She cannot get clerical work here because of her religion; everything is Ku Klux here except the manager and his son.

Nellie Schellinger, also a graduate of Corbin, both girls are converts, the only Catholics in a family of five. She is a school teacher and plans to go to Columbia for an M.A. Both girls plan to get away from Wayland.

Finally, Miss Conroy, who very coolly stepped up to me in the "lobby" last night and introduced herself to me and then introduced me to her multi-millionaire charge, Mr. Fleming, whom she accompanies as nurse. Mr. Fleming is the president of the Elkhorn Coal Co. Though I did not have the pleasure of taking dinner last night with Mr. Fleming, he came over to our table — Mr. & Mrs. Bohannon and myself — and had a little chat. He wears a gold medal of some saint inside his vest. His brother's family is Catholic.

Tomorrow I go to Ligon, Wheelwright and Weeksbury. Instead of going on horse to Ligon, I plan to ride through the mine and then walk six miles, having previously checked my Kit to Weeksbury.

At Pippet Pass, there is a Settlement School, 12 miles from here. I wanted to go up to see it but Mr. Bohannon advised me not to — not by myself. And I didn't want to be contrary, so I yielded. He promised to go with me sometime later. Henry Ford was in Pikeville last Sunday and wanted to get to the Settlement School at Windman but the weather made it impossible. You know how timid I am — at least I am less bold than yourself. It was a consolation for me to read from St. Paul that he worked among the Corinthians "in fear and trembling." I am not physically afraid; I am simply conscious of the fact that I am not wanted around here and I hate to impose upon people. But I do not shirk my duty. I give my life, fruitless as it probably will be, to this work. No, I won't say fruitless; some good is done in a Catholic at the sight of a priest. I don't think I will ever yield to discouragement; of course, my entire outlook may change and discouragement may seize me but the way I feel now, there's nothing to do but show myself, let the world know I'm around. Some day the Church's opportunity may come — in God's good time. Until then, I hope God in His mercy will vouchsafe salvation to these hill-billies; some of whom I am told, spend the entire Sunday in church, taking their lunch with them.

Wayland Hotel- Saturday, October 30, 1926 — 10:00 a.m.

I had to change my plans. I won't see Ligon and Wheelwright today; I hope to see Wheelwright tomorrow afternoon after getting through at Weeksbury.

I found more Catholics at Wayland this morning. One Hungarian family was surprised to find out that they were known as Catholics. I learned of five other families who are Catholic and who don't want it known and I was asked not to go to see them. They are afraid of the Ku Klux. Mrs. Puskas, the mother, cried because she must thus conceal her religion; no holy pictures or crucifix are in evidence in her home; everything is secreted away; the family is awaiting a favorable opportunity to get away, However, the father and mother consented to let two of their children go with two others I found this morning to Estill, Ky. every Sunday afternoon where a Mrs. Music will instruct them for their first communion. That makes a class of six, including two from Estill, that I hope some cold dark early morning will secretly receive their First Holy Communion in some foreigner's humble parlor in Estill.

I had an interesting conversation this morning with a Mr. Galloway who wanted to know whether I knew the Reverend at Lynch. "He sure was mad the day I saw him; he paced up and down the hotel like this and kept saying: "Phew, I'm sore!" He told me more interesting tales about Kentucky, The best I heard at Wayland is this one: as the maid stood at the hotel entrance and rang the dinner bell, a dog began to yowl; she turned to him and said: "What's amatter with you? You don't have to eat this dinner."

Himlerville — Friday, November 19, 1926 — 2:15 p.m.

Two weeks ago today, I wrote a page of my diary; instead of sending it on, I will begin anew. I am in a bad mood for writing but I would rather write herein than do anything else just now.

The next page for your diary should be 81.

I have spent but two nights of this month at Van Lear. The first was when I was called from Covington by telegram on the occasion of the murder of a Pole. No relatives of the dead man have so far been found. On this trip to Van Lear, I found your birthday gifts, which were very appropriate; I am using the gloves continually. From Van Lear I went to Himlerville, then to Ashland to hear the Sisters' confessions, then to Lexington for the conference, then to Covington by bus where we met the following day, as you know. I left for Ashland to examine the school and hear confessions for Fr. Bocklage on Saturday, he staying over in Lexington for a big race. Your train left Covington that night just as I got to the depot. Sunday morning I got to Van Lear at 9:30 and left at 4:30 that afternoon. Such chronicle is anything but interesting; it's like reading a time table but I would like to make a record of it. My destination that night was Louisa, where I met Joe Kuechle, Mat Kramer and Herman Schuler who came for a week's hunting. Monday (November 15) we started early with four Negroes as guides; the Negroes got all the rabbits. I brought back a quart of persimmons, the only thing I was hunting for. It rained and we enjoyed ourselves immensely in maneuvering the Ford back home. We ran out of gas, oil, water and had no chains, so we had to go up the hills backwards and we went sideways almost as much as forwards.

Tuesday I went to Ashland, while the three hunters killed three rabbits, using seven shells on the first one. Tuesday night I was back and we played cards till 5:30 next morning when Joe Kuechle, who had never played cards before in his life, and I went to bed but the others continued till daylight. At 10:30 we left for Van Lear and I tended to some business while two of the hunters made a fruitless hunt.

We all took a twelve hour sleep that night and next day took breakfast in Van Lear, dinner in Louisa and supper in Himlerville, the last lap of our journey being a terrible ride. Three of us had to get out of the Ford to lighten it, while Joe Kuechle pulled it through. Joe said that even a Ford Sedan (we had a touring car) would have been too heavy to get through from Kermit to Himlerville.

This morning, Joe Schuster took us through the mine. After dinner I rode to Kermit with the three, this time the Ford going through with the four of us in it, we going down hill on the return over the worst place. I walked back over the railroad bridge and here I am. I may write again in a day or two.

Van Lear — Saturday, November 27, 1926 — 10:00 a.m.

My bad mood, referred to last time, was due to my running around for a whole week; one night we played cards till 5:30 a.m. I was not with the right bunch to do that.

Wednesday Joe Fedders called at the rectory in Ashland for me on his way to Louisa for his Thanksgiving dinner about 1:30. But I let him go ahead with Sis and Mary Agnes, George and Joe Nabor, Ray Schulte and Charles Castner, and I heard the Sisters' confessions at 3:30, called up Mr. Castner in Huntington and had him pick me up on his way home at 5:00 p.m.

At Louisa we had a gay party, so gay that I said we would not have Mass until seven hours after all had gone to bed. Next morning I said a Mass of Thanksgiving and then joined the men on a hunting party. I remained in the Ford, however, and said my office. In an hour, Joe Fedders came back for me and the other two had gathered over a bushel of butternuts and some beautiful small evergreen trees. I danced around in a creek then but finally went down on the slippery rocks, so I returned at once to Louisa to change clothes. Joe said he would return with the others. Several hours later, the others came back to Louisa without Joe. Joe Nabor went after him and found him leisurely walking towards home.

Friday, yesterday, Joe, Sis and Mary Agnes came with me to Van Lear. It rained almost all day. Now and then Joe and I sauntered out. Philip came home early for the occasion and Mary gave Mary Agnes a dime and wanted Elizabeth to leave her here till Christmas. At 4:30 we four, including Mary Agnes, returned to the Junction. Elizabeth didn't have much to say as train time approached. Finally she said: "I don't see how you can stand it." I didn't feel that way about it then and said so. Then the train came and as we passed the baggage car, we heard one man greet the other, the one asking the other what he was doing in the baggage car and he simply answered, "Got a man in here hurt." All this added to the rain, bad roads, Mary's chatter, etc. was a funny dose for Elizabeth.

Then, back to my taxi. A few moments later, out in the mud, we got a flat tire and no spare! We pulled up to a light and got out and walked up and down on the porch of a country store. And for the first time, did I get a real spell of blues since I am here. Elizabeth's remark is what did it and I kept on repeating: *"Suscipe Domine universam meam libertatem."* When I got home, I said my office and then went to the church for a visit. I have not yet, since I am a priest, found myself in a situation, no matter how difficult, that a fifteen minute visit to the Blessed Sacrament has not composed me.

This morning I went to Dawkins, the station between the Junction and Paintsville, and there met a Mr. Polley, who was waiting for the train to Ashland and Richmond. He had written to me to the effect that Mr. Evans, the general superintendent of the B.S. and K.R. railroad and the big lumber camp at Royalton, would like to have me come to Royalton and preach an "undenominational" sermon. I wanted to talk this over with Polley, hence my trip this morning. My next step will be to take it up with the bishop.

I had intended to answer your fourteen page installment of the diary, but so many things interfered that it finally wore off me. But much of what you wrote is my opinion also, though I would not express myself so vehemently(!) As I told you in Covington, it is my opinion that some bishop made a bad investment. I would say it was in connection with the Archbishop Purcell trouble of some forty years ago when $3,000,000 were lost, but that might be too far back. As for the school and mission collection, I must say, and I know you want me to be plain, I am strong for the idea of training Catholic leaders, no matter what part of the country they will benefit after they are trained. I do not think that Bp. Howard would act like Bp. Brossart did in the matter of a priest's support, now that he has a mission fund. And if help were needed to build a school, I think he would give you the help, but the money would have to be spent according to his ideas and that's where you two would clash. I don't think he would let you put a school up as a whole, in one jump. One of his pet pieces of advice, to me at least, is: let other people think you are dumb. His advice has taken effect and in many of my dealings with him, I "act dumb." I believe that the only way you can get along with Bp. Howard is to recognize his superiority.

From December 2 to 8 I'll be at Himlerville. Please send my page number in care of Joe Schuster.

Himlerville, Ky. — Saturday, December 4, 1926 — 1:50 p.m.

My guess was "School" in answer to your query that I guess the nature of your letter to the bishop, though I failed to mention it in my letter; so I told Joe and Sis on their visit to Van Lear. Do you plan to call on the bishop, as he suggested, after the holidays? I would rather spend a winter week with you in Covington than in Lynch, because I don't like the fifty-two miles of auto travel just now — I don't like it for the sake of the Packard, as well as for my own feelings. Elizabeth is talking about a family reunion at Christmas. Have you heard from her?

I was in Covington for a few days last week, principally because of the Villa Madonna drive which is now under way, with one policy already written up and three more promised. I called on the bishop while in town and he asked me to take a Fr. George Metzler with me to Van Lear and give him something to do. He is a German, in this country for four months, having been expelled from German East Africa by the English. He is 45 years old. I brought him to Van Lear Thursday. I can't find anything wrong with him; one of his first requests was to help him get his first papers for citizenship. Friday morning, I went with him to Paintsville, where he will say Mass Sunday. Upon seeing the town, Van Lear, in daylight, he said, "Oh ho, just like Africa!" So I will now establish my headquarters at Himlerville, with my eye on Stone and Pond Creek, Ky. now being staffed out of Williamson. Every week, for a time, will now see me at Van Lear, Ashland and Himlerville, I still being in charge of the whole territory. Besides, I have business to tend to in Williamson, Royalton, Paintsville and Prestonsburg. I spent only six days of November at Van Lear, twenty days being partly spent on trains and buses.

I am now looking for more suitable quarters at Himlerville, a place where I can put up a desk and a book rack.

My health is as good as it ever was and I now weigh 183-3/4, more than I ever weighed before. I thoroughly enjoy traveling around, though I know I won't like it in summer. In that case, I'll slow down. Almost everyone in the two parties that came up from Covington was knocked out, entirely or partly, by their trip. So I am beginning to wonder whether I ever was a weakling or if it's this life that suits me so well.

While in Covington, I picked up about 60 intentions. I am enclosing a check for ten stipends — *pro uno*. I gave Fr. Metzler thirty. The bishop told me that he had plenty of intentions for me if I wanted them. I have about seventy-five on hand; when will you run short?

Tomorrow I am to take my first lesson on the violin; I wonder if my music will go the way of my Hungarian? Kolos, my teacher, is gone to Cleveland and I have been told by some that it is a most difficult language to master, so I think I'll drop it. If I take up music, it will prevent reading on a big scale, which I am always hoping to begin, but perhaps if I get tired of one, it will always be good to fall back on the other.

I can get you a pedigreed fox terrier, a hound or a German police dog. What do you say?

My new address, simply: Himlerville, Ky.

Himlerville — Tuesday, December 7, 1926 — 12:10 p.m.

Joe Schuster's answer to John Dooley is that the two of them have mutual acquaintances in Lynch and not in Himlerville and so Schuster can say all there is to say in a dozen words. He sends his best regards to Dooley, as well as yourself.

We were told that the Holy Hour could be interrupted by Mass. I see nothing to object to in the first case you mention and I sometimes spend an hour (half-office) in thanksgiving after Mass and often also already spent a part of the hour in preparing my Mass, though, as a rule, I don't "double up" except in one case; the Holy Hour as a thanksgiving after Mass. The second case, that of preparing a sermon, I never could settle for myself and I have never heard an opinion on it. I have often thus made an hour but I have given it up because I find myself preaching to others, instead of being introspective.

We are having quite a cold spell of it here; I am always thinking of Fr. Metzler. I will see him tomorrow night. I. am sorry for him; the elements are not near so severe at Himlerville, because the rooms are smaller and there is a gas heater in every room. So I would not be surprised if he had to give Van Lear up.

I will probably take Kolos' rooms across the street from Schusters: two rooms downstairs. Kolos is giving all of his furniture to the pastor of the place; he owns two good desks, among other things. I'm tired of writing on this page.

Himlerville — Monday, December 13, 1926 — 9:45 a.m.

I made a mistake in exhausting my superlatives some time back when referring to Himlerville mud. It seems now to be 99-44/100 pure mud. I wonder if Lynch ever could have been any worse. And still, we have snow ahead. To my mind, it is a reflection on the inhabitants that they themselves don't solve the problem with stepping stones before their homes. Last summer, some boys repaired a section of the road leading to Schusters so that they could coast down that road this winter. Their work is holding up fine. As soon as I feel enough at home around here, I plan to get these same boys to put stepping stones through the town. One section of the town is passable. By going behind the houses, one can find a walk on the wall built along the creek. But there's a fence right up against the wall so it's pretty hard to navigate when traffic is going in two directions. When passing a young lady, or old, there is only one way for a young man, even a priest, to do it. He must hold on to the fence with one arm as the lady walks into his embrace and then, as he catches on to the fence with the other arm, and she blushingly turns her face away, your, I mean his, lips pass across her cheeks, dangerously close. Luckily I'm above all that, though I have been there!

I meant to write in my diary last night but I was too sour — an eleven hour sleep is making me feel fine this morning.

I had left the little gas stove burn last night in the sacristy, principally to keep the hosts dry. Someone went into the church after me and, in order to save on gas bills, turned out the gas. It's not the first time this was done and I don't know yet who is doing it. But this time I had the gas so low that the cock was almost perpendicular to the gas pipe. The party who put out the gas, first turned off the gas and then pushed the cock over so far that it was parallel to the gas line, thus turning on the gas full force, after having turned it off, just long enough to extinguish the flame. And so gas was pumped into the church full force all night. I wonder how much longer it would have taken for the gas to have become ignited from the sanctuary lamp!

Late this afternoon I leave for Louisa where I will spend the night so as to be ready for Royalton in the morning. I expect to cover Prestonsburg, Van Lear, Ashland and Louisa again this week. I am going to attend a home-talent show at Louisa Friday night. Does it do any good, I am asking myself, to be a good mixer? I stand in with a few non-Catholic families in Louisa and I wonder if I should encourage such relationships. I am going to Louisa

Friday for no other reason than to throw myself among the people and until I see that such a course is fruitless, I will, without forcing it, continue it. I saw Fr. Metzler and Mary last week. Poor Mary! She wants a young priest! She says she is going to move. Fr. Metzler is getting a good dose: seven attended his Mass at Paintsville on his first Sunday; on December 8, at Van Lear, no one was present at Mass. Now for an hour on my violin. I have had two lessons and I am enjoying it.

Himlerville — Saturday, December 18, 1926 — 8:15 p.m.

Some time back, I sat and pondered for some minutes about a school in Lynch and I was tempted for a time to let go in the pages of this diary. How well you sized me up in your last installment! You do not hesitate to unfold a certain line of action even if you realize that you may, before long, be on the other side of the fence. But I don't venture. And so I wrote nothing about a school in Lynch. There was a time when I saw most clearly that there was but one thing to do and that was to organize a school like Fr. Ambrose. I don't mean a boarding school; I mean the way he gradually developed from out of a sacristy school. Today, every advantage I see in a school in Lynch I see is counterbalanced. I am many miles away from your conditions; I don't want to make your problem more hopeless than it is, but I can't find it in me to say "Alfred, go ahead." I am at sea. I would not want to see you undertake a $50,000 job the way you undertook the building of the church and it's not in you to put up a shack! Now, if you were writing this diary, you would write pages about those two sides of the question. I am through; I have no imagination. With me, it's all mathematical, In my sermons, I have but one thing to say. Instead of saying it over in other words, I can say all I want to say in five or ten minutes. I am going to try to overcome that failing by exhausting my subject, as you wrote you do.

It suits me to meet you in Covington a week or two after Christmas, But I will go to Covington December 28 & 29 just the same and get St. John's annual report in shape, at uncle's request, so that when we are both in Covington, the report will take only one day of my time. Uncle will have to shake himself; I had the cash book here for a while and filled out four months' accounts with practically no data to work on,

About that assistant of mine — I don't think the bishop plans to leave him at Van Lear but I do believe that when he finds an opening for him, this territory will be divided.

And now that you know my policy of acting dumb, perhaps you can understand why I have always let you think you could lick me!

My installments often read like a time table. How interesting such reading will be for me later on, I don't know. However, while it is going on —

the running around — I would like to keep a record of my meanderings. The principal events of the week were the taking of a bath and the working out of my first crossword puzzle with the aid of a sympathetic drummer traveling in the same direction as I was. These were the principal events, for one day was spent in visiting a woman in a hospital who had left for home fifteen minutes before I got there and the next day I went to see a man who had died over a year ago!

Monday night I spent at Louisa; Tuesday morning I said Mass at 10:30 at Van Lear, spending the day in answering some mail. That morning at 3:00, an Italian died in a Paintsville hospital, his machine having been hit the day before by an express train. He never asked for a priest, though he called upon Jesus and Mary and was, for that reason, given Christian burial! The mail I had for answering brought a $100 check from the bishop and the first slice of that check is for a bed. Since Fr. Metzler took my former bed, I had been sleeping on a spring patched with boards (while in Van Lear). By lying somewhat crosswise, one could find a fairly comfortable groove. But ever since I slept in that bed, I can't keep myself straight in a civilized bed.

Wednesday, I took the train at 7:20 to the Junction, a second train to Allen, a third one to Martin to see Mrs. Lefsnofski at Martin Hospital. She had just left for Weeksbury; I hurried back to the depot and asked the baggage man if he had a woman on a stretcher. He did. I climbed into the car and began to "parley-vous" when I learned that this party was not Mrs. Lefsnofski; she was in her civvies in the passenger coach; but then I heard a four-blow from the Wayland train and hurried for it because I could get dinner at Wayland. If I went to Weeksbury, I would have to leave again in ten minutes. I did not want to hang around in Martin for five hours.

Everything ran according to schedule till I got back to the Junction at 5:25. I had planned to walk home (3-1/2 miles) in the moonlight but I had a bad headache from too much reading. So I braved a taxi. No closed taxis are running to Van Lear; only machines that are in their second childhood are now on the road. One mile out the fun began: a flat tire. To get the wheel off, the frozen mud had to be cut away from the nuts with a pocket knife. When the wheel was finally off, the owner of the machine (who had just become owner by exchanging an old Ford for his present machine) learned that the spare was mounted on a different kind of rim. By taking three nuts off the other wheels, the owner gathered enough nuts to hold his good tire on. When we got two miles out, the frozen road became so bad (the machine was writhing) that I gave the man a dollar and asked him to let me walk! Oh, my head! But aspirin fixed me up — aspirin bought in Lynch.

The next day I went to Prestonsburg to look up a Catholic chiropractor whose first name was Paul. I asked a man, when I got to Prestonsburg, the way to the court house. He asked me if I was a lawyer; I answered that I was a clergyman. He was a lawyer — Hobson — and invited me to his office and introduced me to his partner, James. The latter didn't know Paul's last name either, but knew that he had died over a year ago. I walked through the town, saw everything, and headed down the track at 10:30, planning to pick up the express somewhere down the line that would pass about 5:00 p.m.! I got to Auxier about 1:00 o'clock and looked up the only Catholic in all the territory I covered so far that day — a son of the Morans you, Philip and I visited in Van Lear. I was going to go to Paintsville from there, but as I started away from Mr. Moran, he asked me where I was going and I said — Van Lear. He said: "It's nine miles that way and two this way," so I went to Van Lear, though it was about four miles and not two, the course taking me through a mine and over a long hill. That night I went to Ashland, working out a crossword puzzle on the train with a drummer who knew Al Moyleben. I slept in a real bed that night after having walked about sixteen miles, Next morning I felt like a springer. I'm going in for more long walks. I hunted me a hair cut after Mass and a shine, bought some film, razor blades, gas stove, broom, etc. and went home and enjoyed a bath, the first one since August, and trimmed my toe nails!

Fr. Bocklage makes it an event almost every time I come to town. We take breakfast about 9:00 and lunch about 1:30. Yesterday, we had oyster cocktail, oyster stew, smoked fish, baked potatoes and cheese pie, together with a bottle of wine, nuts, stuffed dates and candy and a couple of kinds of cheese. Then we both took a nap. I heard the Sisters' confessions at 3:30 and at 4:30 was on board the train for Louisa where I had a complimentary ticket to a show given by the Parent-Teacher Association. It was a fine show — the heroine said to the villain: "Stick your head in a bucket of water three times and pull it out twice." After the show, I returned to Castnor's where, after a couple of hours talk, my day's work was done! Next morning I said Mass at 7:30, giving two Holy Communions. At 8:40, I rushed for my train at Ft. Gay, not dreaming that the Christmas season would probably slow down the train schedule. I waited for the best part of an hour.

And now here I am at 9:40, not anxious to go to sleep. I'll write a letter or two, address some Christmas cards, and think over tomorrow's sermon. I haven't written any sermons for a long time — even at St. John's.

Himlerville — Christmas, 1926 -10:15 p.m.

Do you sometimes think of our first Christmas tree, dad's last Christmas? Christmas makes me blue, it makes me think of St., Charles when the whole kid division pulled away, leaving me alone with three cheers. Do you remember the two apples mother sent us one Christmas, each as big as a football, almost? And the fast day that always had to come on Christmas eve? Then comes to my mind *"Puer natus est,"* the introit of the third Mass; how we were drilled for that Mass at the Cathedral! Finally, mother's last Christmas, five years ago, when you came in on a Monday morning! Christmas, I don't think has passed without tears for ten years. At the seminary, I recall, that I even looked forward to lights out on Christmas eve when I would kneel beside my bed and let the Christmas tears flow! Do you know, Alfred, I believe you would not suffer so much from melancholy if you could cry? Perhaps I am chicken-hearted; I would be effeminate and sentimental if I did not constantly guard my emotions and my words. But when you get what corresponds in my case to blues, you explode; I let off my safety valve. I know you won't adopt my system and I won't adopt yours because you are you and I am I. But I saw Sr. Grace go through a most terrible siege of melancholia and psychoanalysts advised the nuns to induce her to cry; she couldn't for months. Finally, it started — floods of tears — and then she became O.K.

We had a strange Christmas. I made a crib out of a dirty Mason Jar box, covering it with tissue paper and evergreens. By special permission of the bishop, we had a Midnight Mass, a High Mass without *Kyrie, Gloria, Credo, Sanctus or Agnus Dei.* At eight o'clock, we had Mass for the First Communicants. A class of thirty had dwindled down to twelve. At 8:00, only five were in church; I began the Mass at 8:20 with eight children present; two more came late and two others failed to show up. Fifty-seven other children went to Holy Communion. At 10:00, the church was filled again.

I have had a shirt Christmas, a sock Christmas, a muffler Christmas, a cigarette case Christmas — this year was a traveler's kit Christmas. I now have three complete kits and parts galore. Can you use one? Both Noonans and Schusters gave me such a kit. I also have two bathrobes and I would be able to supply you with one — I mean, I would be glad to supply you with one. I don't recall whether you have one or not.

Thursday I was in Ashland to help hear confessions with Fr. Bocklage. I had to go to town in my high shoes, sixteen inches. The track here was under water and I had to go through twelve inches of mud in some places. On this occasion, he gave me a check for $30, asking me at the same time if I would help him out one week in January. I promised him I would. So next week, I'll let you know just when it will be convenient for me to meet you in Covington. Fr. Bocklage served a quail supper Thursday evening.

I'll see Fr. Metzler Monday and he will lay your proposition before his relative in New York immediately. I numbered the last installment of your diary 105 & 106. I hope that the U. S. Steel dividend of 40% is shared by you.

Himlerville — December 31, 1926 — 7:30 p.m.

Everything is topsy-turvy in my rooms. I arrived today at noon and two hours later had all my belongings moved from Oros' to Boyd's, almost directly opposite Schusters. Kolos was the previous occupant of the two rooms that now constitute my home. He left me blankets, sheets, towels, kitchen utensils besides two desks, three chairs, a rocker, a bed, two stoves, carpets, lamps, two bureaus, etc. I am now very comfortably established, Mr. Himler has promised to put in a bath and toilet for me. I hope now to do a little more work at nights. Up until now, I almost invariably spent the evenings at Schusters or Noonans. I am looking forward now to settling down. I have not been settled since I left Covington. I now have plenty of room for all of my belongings and I have already asked Fr. Metzler to send on my books.

I visited Veronica's mother while in Covington. She was doing nicely. Veronica does not know how long she will stay. I told her that Fr. Goebel would like to have me down the week of January 9; if Veronica is not to return by that time, I am sure that uncle would be satisfied if I came down the following week. I don't suppose you would want to leave Rinty alone, would you? If January 16 would not see Veronica home and you don't want to come to Covington till she returns, then I would like to go in on the 9th and again later any time you set. It will take two full days to get St. John's report ready for the printer. If you are in Covington when the report is being prepared, would you mind helping a day? I found on my last trip that the girls who are acting as secretaries at St. John's are way behind in their work.

I am holding Rinty's pedigree for further instructions. Fr. Metzler says wait three weeks and see what his relative's prescription effects. In the event that the results are disappointing, Fr. Metzler said, with a wave of the hand, that you should dispose of the cripple and he would see to it that you got another; also, that a dog with a blemish of any kind was not wanted for breeding. I see Fr. Metzler at least every ten days. If you want direct action, I am sure it would be all right to correspond with him; he appreciated your Christmas greeting, If you wish, you could write to him (in the event you wanted one of his dogs) and say that I told you that he would get you a dog for nothing; that you appreciate this and that your brother knew what kind of a dog you would like to have. This would make the extent of your financial obligation very clear. I am so sorry that Rinty cost you $35 — it never looked that way to me.

I was very much surprised to learn today that Mr. Himler ordered the mine to operate tomorrow — New Year's Day. I had announced Mass at 10:00 and had been told it would be another day like Christmas. Mr. Himler knows that many of the men won't work on a holy day; besides the big coal contracts held by the company will all soon have been filled.

Some day next week I must go to Williamson, W. Va. to see Fr. Gleason who takes care of the Catholics on Pond Creek. I don't know whether I have to include them in my report to the bishop and the government or whether he will do it.

Himlerville — Sunday, January 2, 1927 — 10:45 p.m.

If you want to dispose of Rinty and his sight is not too poor and you have not decided how to dispose of him, you can send him to me. Schuster would be glad to have him for his youngsters and no machines would bother him here. Let me know before Saturday what you intend to do. If you don't know by that time, please don't take any action till week after next.

I have the bishop's report almost ready. I want to enter some records here so that I can look them up next year when preparing the next report so that I may be consistent!

I am reporting 114 families distributed thus; Van Lear — 19, Himlerville — 67, Paintsville — 5, Wayland — 12, Weeksbury — 11. By adding 10% to my actual count, I find 584 souls in the territory assigned to me — the 10% is to take care of the nominal Catholics I have not located. Average attendance at Sunday Mass: Van Lear — 22, Himlerville — 120, Weeksbury — 20, Wayland — 5, Paintsville — 8. The rest I can gather from my cash book. Cash on hand for January 1, 1927 is $8.52.

I have made arrangements to take one meal a day at Schusters and Noonans, alternating every month. My breakfast I intend to prepare myself. I made out an order to Sears-Roebuck today, including wheat granular, rye, cakes, raisins, currents, sauerkraut, pickled. onions, etc. These are only desserts; the body of my breakfast will continue to be raw eggs and milk. I'll soon be hovering around the 200 mark now.

Himlerville — Friday, January 7, 1927 — 12:45 p.m.

It is very unusual for me to feel that I have nothing to do. I feel that free today that the thought of taking a walk up the hill came to me. Only once at Van Lear have I walked simply to walk; and in Covington, about four years ago, I used to take walks. However, I would not be in Himlerville now if I had my C & O pass. To avoid difficulty, the bishop asked to have it sent to Van Lear; Himlerville not being on the C & O. I hope it comes soon. Unless I hear from you that you will be in Covington the week of January 16, I am going to Covington January 9, pass or no pass.

I am now very comfortably settled in my new quarters. I have asked Fr. Metzler to send on the box of books. I did not even unpack at Van Lear. My trunk I will ship through the next time I go to Van Lear.

I do not know yet how much rent I have to pay. My guess is $15. The lady upstairs makes my bed and keeps my rooms clean — a staircase leads from my bedroom upstairs. She also washes my breakfast dishes! I get to my room from the church about 9:00 o'clock; on my desk is a quart cup more than half full of milk. I immediately set to work to fix my breakfast and the fixing consists in lighting the little gas stove and putting the quart cup on it and putting three eggs on my desk. In a minute or so, everything is ready — a breakfast for a king! There is absolutely nothing more that I want, except it be fruit, but that will come in season. I keep a jar of graham crackers on hand, some bran cereal and raisins, simply to vary my diet. After breakfast, I fiddle on my violin till I am sick of it and that is in about an hour and a half. I look upon my violin as my hobby; I have asked myself whether I did not owe it to my calling to make the study of Hungarian my hobby. And I have answered: Hungarian, even in Himlerville, is doomed to die and though I do not wish to hasten that death, why should I aim at prolonging its life? The young folks in the ice cream parlors never think of speaking Hungarian there. I am sure that the children of the present generation will know very little Hungarian. Besides, one must like a hobby. I don't like the study of languages, and I do like music. I had my sixth lesson last night. The violin was given to me by my instructor, a Pole, but I pay $1.00 a lesson and the lessons last from one to three hours.

A great lover of music — and life.

After my violin practice, I turn to my desk and I generally have some correspondence to take care of; then a visit to the church; a little business here and there and then I read till supper time.

7:40 p.m.

My suppers I take at Schusters and Noonans, alternating by the month. With the New Year, I asked both Schuster and Noonan to accept $5.00 a month for whatever meals I took with them. They both very reluctantly yielded to me but had me understand that the $5.00 was not for food and labor but merely to satisfy me. The former arrangement: alternating with the two afore-mentioned families when I came only every two weeks and accepting their hospitality, was all right under those circumstances. But the new arrangement of regular Sunday services may last for ten years.

I received your January 5 installments today. Since you may treat Rinty till the end of the month and therefore may not be in a position to go to Covington even January 16, I'll wire to uncle tomorrow and find out whether it is just as suitable to come to Covington a week or two later as to come January 9th. If he is not ready for me for January 9, I'll put my trip off till January 16 or 23 since you may be able to go to town then — provided Veronica returns by that date. Read the last sentence over and perhaps you will be able to understand it! If uncle has promised the people the report for Sunday, January 16, then I will have to go to Covington next week.

I have felt several times when reading your diary that you were intentionally covering up whatever gay times you were having. What confirmed me in this was the answer you gave to my account of Elizabeth's trip to Van Lear when she so unwittingly started me on the blues. So I was especially glad to read of your Christmas night party. I was glad to read that your usual mood is not the one that so often finds expression in your diary. If the leaves of your diary can serve as a shock absorber, then by all means let them and I will, on such occasions, regard them as such: shock absorbers.

I, on the contrary, write to you frequently about the cheerful side and I hope that the contrast does not make you gloomier — I should have said gloomy. Off and on for ten years I have kept a written record of my examination of conscience; that is, I keep a list of questions which I check myself up on every night. I have recently begun this system again and one of the questions I am now asking myself (I change them every month) is this: Did I play the martyr? I do this to keep myself from talking about what I could regard hardships in my life. I am afraid of making my life hard. For example: I wrote on page 107 that my breakfast was fit for a king. If I told an acquaintance in Covington that I went out for one meal a day and took care of the rest myself by eating three raw eggs and drinking a bucket of milk, I could soon get myself to believe that I had it hard. All this is just in the way of explaining the root of some of my ideas. My system works fine when all is well, physically, mentally, socially, etc. You began that way also; I can make my method more or less permanent because I never stay in one place long enough to get lonesome.

I think I can say that I have become used to my life, so don't be afraid to give me blues. I know conditions in Lynch and there is not so much in Lynch more desirable than what I have here. In fact, I can in all truth say that Himlerville is preferable to all such places where there is but one or two days work each week. About large parishes, I feel that what Bp. Howard said to me is true: "Anybody can run the Cathedral or St. Aloysius or St. John's — almost anybody."

Kolos — the Hungarians pronounce their "s" "eah" — left Himlerville because he was second fiddle on a Hungarian weekly that is steadily declining in circulation. He is now editor of a Hungarian weekly in Cleveland. He was connected with this paper less than two weeks when a Hungarian priest ran away with $1,500 of his money. His position in church affairs here was that of spokesman; another told him what to say — so I am told. However, Fr. Whalen's ways are somewhat antagonistic. It is not natural for him to smile. And so, when upon his recommendation, faculties were withheld from a certain Hungarian priest invited in here by the Hungarians, it looked like a mean thrust from a hard Irishman. It did, however, teach the Hungarians a lesson. A priest wrote to Mr. Himler asking whether he could serve Himlerville on the occasion of Christmas and the letter, in Hungarian, was referred to me. Kolos has been good to me at all times. The furniture he gave me, when new, would cost over $100.

Himlervillle — Friday, January 21, 1927 — 2:45 p.m.

For more than a week have I waited for this opportunity to record events. I returned this noon after having made a run that took me on thirteen trains.

Last Sunday afternoon I buried a man who had shot himself a few days previous. Here alone is material for many pages in my diary: the poor man's suffering from melancholy and depression; the Whalen-tamed Catholics who did not toll the bell until I returned and had given my permission; the large sympathetic crowd that attended the services, held on Sunday because it was urgent to wait no longer. But the climb up the hill with the casket merits a special mention. It was very cold, the last day of our coldest spell; the hillside was steep — 45 deg. angle; the snow was an inch or two deep and slick. It is a corporal work of mercy to bury the dead; it is a prayer to join a funeral procession. Plenty of husky miners followed the bier to relieve the bearers when necessary. Every pallbearer had a man holding his free hand helping him up the slippery hill. Such fraternity is not unusual at funerals, but this was unique. There was no paid funeral director to manage the whole thing; it was through and through a prayer, an act of brotherly love and sympathy for the family of five. At the grave, the men very respectfully disregarding the grief of the wife, solemnly lowered the corpse while the women sang Hungarian funeral songs. The descent from the hill was like the return from Calvary; no autos, or cabs, down the slippery hill in sorrowful procession. The widow will probably be given free rent and work. Himlerville was built, Mr. Himler says, to give the despised Hungarians a home, not to make money. As I came down the hill, I said within myself: "Bury me in Himlerville."

Monday evening I left for Van Lear, spending the night in Louisa. I spent Tuesday, principally, in packing up. Mary is sure that the parish is now going to pieces, quoting all sorts of people. She, herself, will leave the priest house the first chance she gets. But she is sick; she is going to the hospital next week, Fr. Metzler doesn't care if she leaves; he says he can take care of himself. The parish seems to be thriving better under a foreigner than when I was there. More people and more children are attending Mass and instructions than ever before, so Mary's interpretation of events is biased.

Wednesday morning I flagged the train in front of the priest house and Fr. Metzler and I hoisted a 164 pound box of books into the baggage car whose floor was over my head; we got help for the 195 pound trunk. We boarded the same train, bound for Weeksbury where we arrived in about five hours and had a half hour talk with Mrs. Craynor, who is a Watsell, who constitute half the Catholics of Weeksbury. Here the Catholics laugh at the KKK and are unmolested. At Wayland, our destination for that day, the foreign Catholics fear the Ku Klux and so the KKK has a little punch there, We found Mr. Bohannon, the manager, gaining strength. Fr. Metzler had anointed him the week before, He got pneumonia while working in the town when it was under water. Fr. Metzler and I slept in Room 1 in the hotel, over a pool room. Here I took out my alarm clock, which together with my breviary constituted my baggage, distributed in my overcoat pockets. I had an opportunity to see how Germans dress. Fr. Metzler wore, besides his overcoat and heavy suit, a black shirt and then another shirt, large and heavy, reaching to his knees; heavy under-wear and stockings, not socks.

Fr. Metzler will say Mass at Weeksbury every third Sunday and at Wayland every fifth Sunday.

At 5:20 next morning, our train left for Allen when Father and I parted; he going on to Covington and I to Pikeville. I had a four hour wait at Allen and most of this time was spent in conversation with a 45 year old Red Man, Odd Fellow and KKK. He told me, rather apologetically explaining that he was brought up thus, that he doesn't smoke Camels because one cent from every pack sold goes to the "pope in Rome." I learned further that the majority of Jews are Catholic, that Catholics don't believe that Christ has come, that they believe that their "pope" is God, We became good friends. for the time. There are thirty-two denominations, according to John Sherman Gibson Adams (his mother Gibson must have some Indian in her because Gibson is an Indian name) and the furthest away from the Bible are the Holy Rollers. At Pikeville, I was very cordially received at the hospital where I went to visit a Mexican who broke his back a year and a half ago. He is being well cared for, physically. Every once in a while, they pack him into an ambulance and take him to the Methodist church. He, however, knows his religion and only tolerates such action. I left a rosary with him which he gratefully accepted. He is 26 years old, gets $15 a week compensation and worked in Lynch a few months prior to his accident.

Then, a six hour run to Ashland, picking up the Mass kit at Paintsville and leaving it at Louisa. I left Ashland at 5:45 this morning and said Mass in Louisa, getting my train at Ft. Gay at 8:50. From Louisa I took with me a heavy suitcase which I had previously checked to that point and, after picking up two more bundles at the Kermit express office, I was loaded down for my walk to Himlerville.

My life, I think, is in danger every time I pass through Warfield, Ky. on foot. This morning, as I was walking down the railroad track on the West Virginia side, just before coming to the railroad bridge which I cross into Kentucky, I was assailed by the vilest epithets from the Kentucky side. A dozen times, at least, I was called a God-damn-son-of-a-bitch; Hunk; was told to go to hell and all this in a terrible rage. For the first time on such occasions, I stopped and tried to identify the owner of the voice, I could not see him but was told that I would certainly know him when we met. This is the third time that I am sure of that this abusive language was meant for me, but it has never taken place at close range. Once when passing a group of six or eight men at rifle practice in Warfield, one man suggested to "make this guy the target." This, of course, was in jest, but meant at my expense. I am not afraid of my life, And, this may seem silly, but here it comes. I am going to do nothing to provoke these people and I am wishing a martyr's portion! I only hope that the guy who shoots me won't be drunk and that, if there is a shooting, it is done out of hatred for my priesthood. Nor do I write this that I wish a martyr's crown, that others may praise me, but that God may be praised and glorified by the blood of a Kentucky missioner. No! I'm not dead yet; but there's a chance!!!

And when I returned, I found that my bed had been on fire. The girl from upstairs had lit my gas stove a few days ago to dry out the room, and was a little careless.

I intend to take Mary Verbonic to St. Elizabeth's Hospital Monday. Monday night, I expect to leave Covington for Lynch and hope to bring with me an apology from Elizabeth; a letter from her told me of the spat. Perhaps I'll arrive before this.

Himlerville — Tuesday, February 8, 1927 — 11:00 a.m.

The last time I wrote to you I spent an hour or two in writing. I am beginning this with a feeling that I have not a thing of interest to inscribe and I can't see myself writing for an hour or so this time. Ah — an idea! I'm beginning to thaw!

I remarked once before that a trip to Lynch was the most enjoyable I ever had. I can say that about my recent trip again. I weighed myself at Van Lear Junction while waiting for a train and to play a little trick on myself (after my return from Lynch). I weighed myself, smiling, with my overcoat on. I was stunned — 194 lbs! I took my overcoat off, took my breviary out of my pocket and took off my smile and weighed in again. I then read 187-1/2. Then I realized that my collar was tight around my throat.

I took Mary Verbonic to the St. Elizabeth's Hospital last week. The previous week she disappointed me by not showing up in Ashland. This time she appeared nervous and scared, without any breakfast, hoping she would not find me at Ashland. But she did. The first night in Covington she spent with Elizabeth. The next day she was put in the tubercular ward; the day following, she was taken out for there was no trace of tuberculosis for which she had been doctoring for two years. They will keep her under observation for a while and give her imagination a rest.

Upon my return from Covington, I found a check for $250 from Bp. Howard in my mail. In acknowledging it, I told him that I hope Himlerville would be self-supporting in two or three years. However, since Kolos left, the finance organization has been crippled. The vice-president has come to me now several times asking financial advice (Kolos is still nominally president). This is just as I want it; eventually I want to control all the moneys. So we have planned together several doings. I have written and asked Mr. Cella, a sort of a magician, to come to Himlerville for a performance. In May we have planned an outdoor picnic and I hope to introduce a raffle wheel-; if not at that time, then in September at some indoor festival. Besides this, we plan to call together about fourteen of the most influential Catholics and explain the envelope system to them and let them do the *right kind of talking* for a week or two and then these same fourteen, seven teams of two, call on every wage earner on a selective basis — that is, each wage earner will be approached by the team most apt to have some influence on him. I am asking for ten cents a day for every day the donor works, or fifty cents for a full week, but they say I am shooting too high. We will see. At present, on the fifty cents a month plan, collected every three months, only the fathers of families are asked to contribute, whereas there are a good number of single fellows who would give as much and more if approached by the right man or team. The Sunday collection at present averages less than $10 a Sunday. I also proposed to the vice-president (Mr. Yuchasz) that I urge a big Easter and Christmas collection. He was not in favor of the Easter collection because about at that time a Hungarian priest will come to Himlerville and every Hungarian will give at least a dollar. I am confident that Himlerville can become self-supporting but uneducated people, I have learned, get some bum ideas once in a while and funny notions sometimes go through the camp. For example: I am now saying two Masses every Sunday. I explained to the children at the early Mass that their obligation of hearing Mass was satisfied. One man, the secretary, came to me, indignant, and requested that I should not instruct the children that it was not necessary to come to 10:00 Mass.

Himlerville — Saturday, February 12, 1927 — 8:00 p.m.

Once more I can record progress; it's encouraging to see things moving no matter how slowly they move. Today I found that it had been made possible to light the entrance to our church. It may seem small to rejoice over such an insignificant event but I am glad just the same when there are signs of life.

It takes so long to get things done in a mining camp. The classic example for these parts is the repairing of the roof of the Van Lear priest house after seven years of waiting. I had a bookcase made at Van Lear that took me to the carpenter shop a half a dozen times; it finally arrived after I left Van Lear. It took four days to get a plumber to repair an ice-broken water pipe. In Himlerville it is no different. I asked for a toilet to be put into my quarters on January 3. The room has been built — that is, the carpenter is through — but last week the bowl and water basin had not yet been ordered. I also asked for a bookcase; it has been promised me and I'll be satisfied if I get it some time this coming summer. So it is in China, I am told! And so it happens that I have many hopes sprouting; I am confident that most of them will materialize. Since before I came to Himlerville, a certain group has been "getting'" a rubber runner for the center aisle of the church; I have been promised a homemade vestment case; I have been asked to price baptismal fonts — by an individual, not by the "board;" someone else wants to give two more boys' surplices. I hope after that to get two parlor chairs for the sanctuary (the servers now sit at the feet of the priest preaching, facing the people); also six balanced candle holders — I now have three pair, selected and contributed by three different people with anything but similar tastes. Then all I will want will be a droplight in each of the two sacristies, and some day, perhaps, a custom-made confessional, though this is not as necessary as a liturgical altar.

The big thing that is simmering though is the future Catholic-public school. I had requested our bishop to obtain for the mayor of Himlerville an opinion from the attorney general of Kentucky regarding the standing of nuns teaching in the public school of Kentucky; nuns, of course, holding state certificates, Today's mail brought this from Bp. Howard: "I am advised there is no law that forbids the authorities to employ the teachers mentioned. When you come to Covington, I will give you full information in regard to the matter." Perhaps this is the beginning of all sorts of scraps, with the Catholic Hungarians for not getting Hungarian nuns; with the Presbyterian Hungarians for proselytizing; with the natives who are attending but who won't have anything to say; with the county authorities who hate the Hungarians and their religion (so I am told); then, I am never sure of our mayor, Noonan, who as a brother K.C. I hope to get his cooperation. Finally, Mr. Himler might upset the whole works for his dream of nuns in Himlerville was a dream of Hungarian nuns doing social work among Hungarians. But it's a beautiful game; I have plenty of time a-riding the trains to figure out whose move it is next.

I am making arrangements to bring the Eucharistic Congress film to Himlerville. It can be had for 15 cents for every person seeing the picture; the renter charging whatever price he pleases.

Himlerville — Tuesday, March 1, 1927 — 11:30 a.m.

Every once in a while I make some progress — honest! But, there are loads of things that I put off until such a time as when sisters will be in Himlerville and I am still fondly hoping that next September will see them here. But as time goes on, the difficulties seem greater in the way of bringing them here. So every once in a while, I have to make a move without counting on sisters. A game of marbles in the church during Mass helped me to make up my mind on one point in a hurry: community prayers during Mass for the children present and about thirty are now present daily. I have no Mrs. Murphy to help me out and right now something is wrong with my principal assistant, Miss Monarch — the only Catholic school teacher here. She failed to show up two Saturdays in succession for her catechism class and doesn't even come to week-day Mass any more. So I have to fall back on my servers. At certain parts of the Mass, I'll have one of them read aloud certain prayers and eventually I'll get all the children to pray aloud together.

Tomorrow, Ash Wednesday, I will distribute blessed ashes; this will be the first time 95% of the children witness this ceremony. Friday night, Himlerville will have the Way of the Cross for the first time, followed perhaps by benediction — I can't decide so many things at once!

I am still waiting for half of last year's salary. It is now in the bank but no one here seems to have any authority to draw it. In the beginning, I was told I would have it on the last day of the year (1926); then I was told that I would get it before January 15 — the day I wanted to send my report to the bishop — then Kolos wrote he would be in Himlerville on January 29 to sign my salary check and preside at the meeting that was to elect his successor. Nor did he come on February 13. After that, a notice was posted that

Kolos or no Kolos, the meeting would be held on February 27 at 2:00 p.m. in the school building. On February 26, Kolos wired that he would surely come on March 6. The meeting was again postponed. Many things waiting for my important decision are awaiting the installation of the new board! If the new board is ever elected and we get nuns in here, there will be enough decisions decided to make a regular parish out of this place. These are some of the things pending: a deed to the church property giving the Bishop of Covington the title to it; this necessitates the release of the lease held by the Himler Coal Co. and a transfer from the owner Berger, a Cincinnati Catholic, to the bishop, as well as the surrendering of the building on the property. The bishop will be responsible for the debt and then come down the state (or up the river) and bless the property and give it a name. Then I want complete control of the finances and an envelope system. Then will come a vestment case, a confessional, a baptismal font and, eventually, a new altar and a statue or two and an electric light in the sacristy. But the school is the big thing I want and if I can't get that, I'll try a public high school, with myself as principal (being registered in Frankfort as a recognized teacher in a recognized college) and if that doesn't work, by gosh we'll go after a private high school!

Himlerville — Saturday, March 5, 1927

I am completing my first full week entirely spent in Himlerville; I did not even go to Ashland to hear the Sisters' confessions. On Monday I felt very uneasy about the prospect of spending a solid week in this hole among the hills, but I clinched my teeth and with a set jaw was determined to hold myself here for ten days to get used to the place if for no other reason. But there were other reasons, principal among which is that one of my offices is to live among these people and be a leaven in the pot. But I had a struggle Monday — I just spent two successive weeks in Covington and that looked like laying down on the job. So I tried to get myself back into harness. I will not now go over the chronology of the week; I am glad I did not run away. I am as happy in my work tonight as I ever was. And that's what I want to write about. If I thought I would make you blue by what I have to say about my work, I would hold out these pages till the bulk of my diary comes back to me and then put them in their chronological place. But I believe you would be glad to see me contented as I am glad, not only to have you write to me of your dark moments but of the bright ones as well.

I finished hearing confessions at 7:45, having previously swept a week's dried mud out of the church. Fourteen girls came to confession. I expect ten more tomorrow, it being the first Sunday — girls' Sunday. After I locked up, I picked my way across the muddy road, with the aid of my flashlight, and stood on the store platform and looked the town over, as much of it as I could see. The streets were deserted; some people were at the show, I suppose, others in the "Parlor" (our principal refreshment parlor), and the others at home. I thought of the mining towns we used to pass through on the C & O on our way to St. Charles. How they used to frighten me at the thought of living in such a place; the houses were creosoted, the children and pigs shared the same recreation grounds, the cows seemed so forlorn in the grassless, sooty, musty streets. I suppose Inman, Va. is a good sample of what I thought a coal camp was from what I saw of them from the C & O train. And the coke ovens! Who wanted to live in a place like that? If a fairy would have told me that in such a place was I to do my work, my spirit would have been crushed.

Tonight I stood on the store platform and thought of these things and, by the grace of God, I was strangely happy. True, the pigs are penned up here and the children are cleaner and brighter than the children of natives, but it's a hole just the same, several miles off the main track, not an automobile moving this year yet and it being necessary to bring the mail through with a four-mule wagon. As I strolled to my rooms, I thought of what my presence means to these people. Here, in a Catholic colony, a priest is in an Acadia; these children I know are mortifying themselves more than the children of St. John's did during any Lent that I knew them. Tonight I am glad to be here and I can do more good here than a man who would not like to be here. Here, a priest must become of the people; he must make this his home and want to stay here indefinitely.

I was dirty from sweeping the church, and thirsty, and so I went to the well with my pitcher and even now yet have several hours for writing and reading.

My thoughts continued to run along. As Fr. Tappert has become identified with Mother of God's parish and uncle with St. John's and Fr. Poole with Verona, so I think I will become identified with Eastern Kentucky. I don't think I will stay in Himlerville all my life, but I do believe I will be around here some place for a long time. I hope, within the next two or three years, that the bishop will have a church built in Paintsville or in Louisa, or in both places because these places are centers and I have learned that there are many Catholics passing through these towns and many others would settle if there were a Catholic church around. Bp. Howard is of the opinion that if a church were built in Paintsville, Catholics would come from everywhere. Paintsville is the Lexington of Eastern Kentucky, not the Harlan of your district.

I am going to make fewer trips to Covington. I promised Julitta Burkard that I would be at the Villa for her reception into the Benedictine Order. But for that, I would not go to Covington before Easter.

Tuesday I will give Robert Vastner his first lesson in Latin, in preparation for his entrance into the Latin School next September. This will take me to Louisa. Wednesday I shall go to Huntington to visit one of our men in the hospital; the same night I will preach in Ashland. Thursday I'll go to Van Lear. So you may not hear from me for more than a week.

Himlerville — Monday, March 14, 1927 — Noon

I have written to Fr. Metzler about Fr. Mike and will let you know what arrangements suit him best at the end of the week. However, I know that the first week after Easter would suit him best because that happens to be the fourth Sunday of the month and on the second and fourth Sundays, Fr. Metzler is at Van Lear. I may see Fr. Paschal next week.

I have noted what you write regarding your insurance and St. Charles. It's kind of you to include me as benefactor. My days of giving financial help are over — for the present at least. I have given away less than $10 since my appointment to Eastern Kentucky. I am not getting it to give.

I have promised some boys to do a trick or two for them. Will you please send on the three red balls, chain and lock and a couple of the other deceptions?

The pendulum of my influence has been swinging to and fro since the beginning of this year. And it is interesting to watch the process. I smile through it all, never once being carried off by glee or ruffled by a dig, because almost invariably is there a reaction when the pendulum is anywhere but in dead center. A week ago yesterday, Kolos appeared on the scene. He called a meeting in the afternoon which I attended. It was an endurance test; each one remained as long as he could stand it. I sent a messenger to Noonan's and told them not to wait for me for dinner and I was the sixth from last to leave the school room where the meeting was held. Practically all the business was carried on in Hungarian. For a half hour, Kolos spoke of Fr. Whalen, Fr. Hern, Fr. Hanses. Then came the elections for new officers. There were no nominations and ten offices to be filled, with the result that the votes for the worthy ones were scattered over several offices and, in one case, a man, who never attends church, was elected to two offices. The first vote cast for the office of collector was for me; these keen-sighted people have already discovered my ability as a financier! I was defeated for the office of trusteeship but was successful in outrunning four other contestants for the office of president and thus, for a few moments, became Kolos' successor! I made a little speech of resignation while at the height of my popularity and my words were translated. Evidently that was just what a half a dozen wanted, each one of whom wanted the job. When finally one man was agreed upon for the presidency, I sailed in; about ten of the original thirty-five members of the meeting having left. (Of these 35, 9 voted for me for president.) I wanted two things: an envelope collection and the deed to the church property. I was told I would get both, but we ought to have another meeting!!! It was finally decided to discuss these two questions at a meeting of officers on the following Sunday (yesterday). Five of the ten were present. I called the meeting and for fifteen minutes a word battle in Hungarian went on. I learned last night what it was about; the vice-president told the president that his, the vice-president's, job was to watch the president because he had Americanizing tendencies. Finally, I butted in. I got what I wanted: an envelope collection without submitting it to a general election. Immediately I outlined a beautiful plan: seven teams of two men each to canvass the parish. I was told to do it myself. Two men volunteered to go with me. The question of getting a deed to the property giving the bishop title to it was laid over to another meeting.

I had a good talk with Mr. Himler this morning. He was not as uncomfortable in my presence today as he was on other occasions. I spoke to him about getting control of the church property, to protect Catholic interests in case the coal company ever changed hands. Kolos at one time had given the Presbyterians permission to use the church building for their services and it was on Easter. With the minister in church, ready to conduct the services, and Mr. Himler attending, the vice-president raised so much hell that the service was called off. Kolos had dreams of fraternalism. I had this in mind when I spoke to Mr. Himler. He told me plainly that at one time he wanted to keep control of the property because he was afraid the Church might use her offices to injure him. While Fr. Hern was giving a mission here, a movie was going on. Fr. Hern, infuriated, raved that if such a thing happened in another coal camp, the people would mob the theater. But since the bishop was here, he, Mr. Himler, is satisfied to let him have control. My appointment followed only a few weeks after the bishop's visit. I wonder if Mr. Himler knew that Fr. Whalen was to be changed! Fr. Whalen had no trouble with Mr. Himler but Mr. Himler and Kolos and several others could not pull with Fr. Whalen.

The postmaster is facing a penitentiary sentence for opening a registered letter; the banker is going to quit; the town recently was out of bread and it was rumored that the baker quit, but he was only drunk. A miner was fired and he is taking several sympathizers with him.

Himlerville — Sunday, March 27, 1927 — 8:30 p.m.

I have lost track of the page numbering again.

Fr. Pascal told me that he could not come to Himlerville till about the third Sunday after Easter. Fr. Metzler doesn't feel the need of a Polish priest at Van Lear, since there are no Poles there who cannot understand him. I hope you won't find it embarrassing to cancel whatever arrangements you might have made with Fr. Mike about Van Lear.

I am working at two major propositions: a title to the property on which the church stands, and nuns for Himlerville.

The Himler Coal Co. holds a lease to the desired property. At the time of Fr. Hern's visit here, Mr. Himler was determined never to let the control of the church property out of his hands; the bishop's visit last July changed his attitude. The company leased the property from O. L. Burger, Cincinnati and Mr. Himler informed me that Mr. Burger would give me no trouble. I went to see Mr. Burger last week. He was surprised to learn that there were buildings on his property. He owns 900 acres of coal land in Martin County; this was leased to the Himler Coal Co. After mining 44 acres, the company gave it up as a profitless field and have notified the owner that they want to surrender their lease for at present they are still paying $6 an acre minimum royalty. Burger wants the company to make some cordrills (I'm not sure of the spelling) to see whether the coal is any better beyond their place of last occupation. The company wants Burger to make the cordrills. In the meantime, the company runs into a good six foot stretch of coal on another lease and now is not anxious to work Burger's lease in any case. Their original lease from Burger was for fifty years. While working his forty-four acres, the school, the bank and the church were built on his surface — built in good faith. Now they want to give up the lease and I spilled the beans when I told Burger about our church on his property. I did not tell Himler that I was going to speak to Burger; my only thought was to make my visit to Burger only a preliminary step. Burger was very nice to me; he said his troubles with the coal company would not involve me and asked me to set a price for the property I wanted. I told him I would write, I did not want to go any further when I realized what I had done. Sooner or later, Burger would have been informed of the situation because Himler is fair and square. I have asked Noonan to take off the property I want, to locate it for me on paper and then I was going to go to Himler and ask him to let me proceed. But Noonan thinks he knows a better way out of it — so I'll wait a while.

About nuns. My first dream was to get a couple of nuns hired as public school teachers. The bishop consulted Galvin who got an opinion from the attorney general that Kentucky Law did not prohibit nuns to teach in the public schools, but the attorney general added that the local boards could cause all sorts of trouble. Mr. Himler advised to wait till after the next legislature when he was confident that the coal companies would be able to have such a law enacted that would take the schools in certain districts (coal mines, for example) out of the control of the county board. That looked too thin to me and so I schemed for a private high school. Two years ago,

Himlerville was fighting for a high school. I had my eye on the tennis court that no one uses any more and asked the bishop whether he would finance a Catholic High School in Himlerville. It was at dinner table at Villa Madonna, his answer was: "That proposition would interest me." But on my return to Himlerville, I learned that there would only be six or eight Catholics eligible and it would be problematical whether others would attend. There were other difficulties in the way and so my second scheme gave way to a third. Now I am dreaming of getting some nuns to Himlerville for a summer course. My plan includes these points: half hour of study in the school building, followed by about forty-five minutes of recitation, this to be followed by an hour of sewing for the girls and perhaps drawing for the boys. On some days we could have singing instead; on other days, a picnic. In the afternoon, the girls could work with the nuns on their sewing if they wished but, of course, there would be no school after 10:00 a.m. or thereabouts. However, I almost have to have a Hungarian nun for prejudice sake. I intend to write to the Benedictines today and ask them to have some Benedictine community farm a Hungarian nun to them for six weeks.

Monday — 12:45 p.m.

The new president, Mr. Hauser, asked me this morning when the Hungarian priest was coming. I answered: "Three Sundays after Easter," to which he answered: "We don't want him then. I'll write to Cleveland today for a Hungarian priest and have him send on his credentials at once. We want the priest on Easter."

This morning I administered Extreme Unction for the first time in Eastern Kentucky. I had to work with an interpreter.

Last Thursday I was introduced to the man who built the road through Himlerville. He seems prosperous, evidently everything he tackled he made a success of.

Himlerville — Saturday, April 2, 1927 — 8:30 p.m.

As I often do, I left a whole lot to be surmised in my note to you recently. What I meant was this: I have often looked through novelty catalogues but always felt that their line seemed so cheap. The ladies of St. John's suited my taste better by buying in Cincinnati, by buying stuff I did not see listed, by buying without any instructions whatever, other than this — that we wanted articles to sell at 5 cents and 10 cents a catch, we to realize from 50 to 100% profit. To make you rest at ease, because yours is a big undertaking, let me suggest this: that you send me the $40 and I'll spend it as you outlined and I'll fix it up with uncle that anything you cannot dispose of you can send to him for his picnic — then the ladies can buy with Lynch in mind and with St. John's in the background. I never paid very much attention to what they bought but I remember that there were polychrome rubber balls, rubber balls with a long "come-back" rubber attached, peacock whistles (by putting water in these whistles and then blowing them, the sound gurgles), besides a lot of perfectly useless stuff that the kids went crazy for. We never went too far with our fish pond, why let the children spend all their money on such stuff is what we figured.

Paddle tickets cost about $1.50 a hundred for 60 tickets 60 numbers (that means one number to a ticket). They are little cheaper if ordered 30 tickets 60 numbers — 2 numbers on a ticket.

Wouldn't it be grand if Fr. McCrystal and Metzler and myself could all come to Lynch together sometime for, say, two days? But not at your bazaar; some other time. I'll let you know later whether I can come at that time. I had another thing on my mind that week of which I'll write later.

Himlerville — Friday, April 8, 1927 -8:45p.m.

Today I was called upon to baptize a dying infant, a child of non-Catholic parents. I just completed my sixth letter to the bishop this week; in one I asked for $250, in another for $1,000, in another for faculties for a Cleveland Hungarian priest, in another I reported regarding Paintsville from where I had just returned. In answer to my request for $1,000, I was told that the bishop would allow that sum for one year in the event that I opened up a High School in Himlerville. The matter is still in the air. Today I learned that our Altar Society did not have enough money in the treasury to pay for a year's supply of sanctuary lamp candles because, under pressure of one of our Catholics, they had contributed $35 to a Protestant orphanage in the poverty stricken Hamlet of Philadelphia. Today was also memorable because I was promised, promised — mind, no more, a raise in salary. I asked for $25 a month plus rent $15 which will constitute a raise of $15. It sure must be hell to be a Sulpician and live on 15 cents a day! I thought I had learned frugality at the seminary when I washed my own socks and handkerchiefs, but later learned new ways of saving when I was $2.00 in the hole — that's when St. John's paid the nickel car fare or the gallon of gasoline when I went on a sick call. Now I'm a novice in a school in which some folks with a laborer's income and a large family can build up a bank account of $5,000. I don't want to seem pessimistic, but if it would not be for Bp. Howard, I would have to find a sideline like teaching.

Fr. Metzler can't take my place at the Cathedral on Holy Thursday, so I'm going in Thursday morning. Ship your oil stocks to me please in care of Fr. Bocklage Tuesday or to uncle; if you send to me in Covington, the postmaster may send them to Van Lear. Also send on your bazaar order, if you wish.

Himlerville — Easter, April 17, 1927 — 3:15 p.m.

I am sincerely sorry for having caused you additional mental anguish, because I had a sneaky feeling that I was asking something unreasonable, knowing as I did the make-up of Lynch Council. I hope you sent the New York dog back. I am going to Covington next week. If there is anything you want me to do for your bazaar, address me hereon as you did last week.

Marcella Seiler, a girl from St. John's, will make vows at Maryknoll on April 30. I promised her a half year ago to come to see her at that time. However, it is on a Saturday, so I next promised her to leave here on May 1, Sunday. On May 5, I have to be in Ashland, which suits me just right. I don't like to stay around a convent too long. I would not like to postpone my visit again, especially since it seems that more of her folks from Covington will be present for the occasion. This was the principal reason why I did not promise definitely to come to Lynch that week. I have not shipped your bats yet but you will get them next week.

I thought I might write about ten pages at this sitting but I'm too tired. About 160 received Holy Communion this month; twelve received their First Holy Communion. Fr. Unger from Cleveland is here; he is Mr. Himler's guest. I took dinner with him today. He seems O.K. The least thing can upset Himlerville. Fr. Unger must have been tipped off by some busybody that a certain person was coming to confession. I had had her marriage validated with a Sanatio and she had been to confession to me and to Holy Communion. Fr. Unger refused her absolution and she kept the matter no secret. Then she came to confession to me and received Holy Communion this morning after I explained the situation to Fr. Unger. But the burg is dizzy. My only explanation is that the bishop did not find it necessary for the parties concerned to remarry. Next Saturday, by special permission, I shall officiate at a mixed marriage with Mass, but it is never to happen again at Himlerville.

Himlerville — Tuesday, May 10, 1927 — 11:10 a.m.

Everything is sailing smoothly. I hope it will continue so for a long time to come. I visited all of the Catholics on Easter Monday and Tuesday, tried about a dozen different concoctions and left a box of weekly envelopes at each home. Mr. Yuhasz acted as interpreter. I became a yes-yes man. Mr. Yuhasz offered me a drink of dew before we started but I declined because I wanted to keep my tank empty as long as possible. O.K., said Mr. Yuhasz, but he had to take one so that he could talk better! Everybody we visited was in an excellent mood! I was told what a wonderful priest I was, with an arm around my neck several times. Easter Monday is the day to visit Hungarians. Our collection immediately mounted from $13 a Sunday to $25. I left one box at each house. A committee now is asking every wage earner to take a box of envelopes.

Our debt is now $800, my salary now is $40 a month, $15 of which goes for rent. We are now planning a picnic for July 4th. A few years ago, such a picnic netted $350. It was preceded by a parade of four automobiles and eight bicycles and a band. All bicycles have since disappeared. In the fall, we plan a big dance and then a big Christmas collection. As soon as the debt is paid, I want $100 a month salary, but no one knows that yet.

Kermit High School was closed last week and the board forced to retire. The new board, with no money, has repudiated the old board's debts. A truant officer had been getting $360 a month; all the members of the board enriched themselves. But the teachers have only "claims." And now, all this talk of a Catholic High School in Himlerville is gradually getting around.

Himlerville — Sunday, May 15, 1927 — Noon

I was very much relieved when I read your last installment. Rinty has not yet been heard from — I think he has been stolen.

I am waiting for the roads to open. I have a few trips planned with oil men and an engineer but the weather has been terrible. The Lynch road is not open yet, is it? When it opens, how about my coming to Lynch for a couple of days? How about having Fr. Metzler and McCrystal over for two nights and I with them and then before the end of the summer, I would like to come over by myself. If you are afraid to tackle such a proposition, I'll promise to go on a diet! I would invite you to Himlerville but, first of all, I can travel cheaper than you and then when you land here, you are here and that's all. Even the wine I have is the rottenest I ever tasted. I got a batch of grape juice from Burkart (Jr.) and it certainly did not come up to specifications. The keg was from Cleveland, some sodium in it, whereas I was told that it would come to me packed in ice, free from all preservatives. It was not packed in ice. From my experience, I would advise you to buy Stetter's Concord if you want to try it some time. But it's expensive — less than $2 a gallon — no, it's more than $2 a gallon if you add on the freight and sugar.

Don't say come till the roads are in shape. I can't come the week of May 29. Srs. Domitilla and Vincentia are going to look Himlerville over some time during that week and the question of a High School in Martin County will be settled one way or another within a month.

Kermit's twenty-second residence within a year was destroyed by fire a few days ago. The insurance companies are planning to cancel all policies.

Dennis Noonan won the K.C. auto. I have the use of it whenever I want it — but why want it — in Himlerville?

Louisa, Ky. — Thursday, May 26, 1927 — 11:15 a.m.

I landed here at 11:00 a.m. yesterday, ate an egg sandwich and went to bed. Robert Castner took my suit to the cleaner who said he would have it done before night. He sent it at 11:00 today, just as my train pulled in at the depot. I missed it. The N & W from Ft. Gay to Cattletsburg will get me to Ashland in time to hear confessions this afternoon for the opening of Forty Hours Devotion.

We left you on the Virginia-Kentucky line, as you know, at 3:30 yesterday morning with our trousers rolled up high. We had about two miles to go to get to our train and before we got it, I wished that I had heeded your suggestion and had gone back with you and taken the 400 mile route instead. We started down the mud, swinging the flashlight, one flash of light before me, one behind me for Fr. Metzler. All would have been well but I yielded to Fr. Metzler's insistence and we branched off the road along one of the several paths into the woods. Fr. Metzler took me off the road and I got back at him by losing the path. And there we were on a mountain side, before crack-o-day, in a woods and lost! Neither blamed the other but both worked hard to get out. Fr. Metzler would stand where he was and I would go ahead for some thirty feet and explore with my flashlight. Then he would make for the light. We first attempted to reach the gully, always working towards our left — the direction of Jenkins. But we had to give it up. As time sped by and the thought of missing our train kept coming to me, I had to call on my will power to keep from getting panicky. The best way I can describe my feelings is to state that I was ready to sit right there in the intermittent rain and wait for daylight. But just then Fr. Metzler took the lead. Our course now took us straight up hill to get back to the road. Towards the end, had no idea whether we had five yards or two hundred yards to go. But up we went, over fallen trees and through bushes, once picking ourselves up and then our grips. At 4:25 (train left at 5:00), I almost whimpered. We saw the road when it was about four feet from our eyes — the last fifty feet went up a bank at an angle of more than 45 degrees. Fr. Metzler was going like a man accustomed to jungles, as he is.

As we started down the road, wet from rain and perspiration, my collar in my pocket, my glasses also, the dawn began to streak the sky. I suppose the scenery was beautiful. We thought of only our train. And I thought afterwards how close we might have been to snakes such as we saw going up that same road Monday morning. In the woods I heard nothing but a few frightened strange birds. I wonder how snakes act in the dark.

If I had been alone, I would have had no fear of missing our train, but Fr. Metzler held us back. He traveled more like a tractor; on the hill side he made as good time as I did, but on the open road, he did not have as high a speed gear as I did. But we kept going; there must have been about two miles to go, through mud, most of it. If I had taken your atlas along, it would have gone the way of excess baggage! When we reached a sidewalk, I stamped my feet to dispose of another class of excess baggage. Then I realized how weak my knees were, for I reeled from the stamping.

Down, down the grade we went, faster and faster. Around the bend came a view of the steam from the safety valve of our locomotive all ready to go. We had a half a minute to make it. Fr. Metzler couldn't run; he was as wet as a mop. Then the locomotive bell chimed and off it started. I ran; Fr. Metzler did the impossible and started after me. I jumped a platform and rounded a hedge and didn't know what to do. I could hop the running train, but Fr. Metzler? The engineer saw me and nodded and stopped the train! Those on the train were too sleepy to notice us; the conductor was sympathetic. Fr. Metzler opened his window; he had to, he said, and no wonder! He went to the smoker to change his shirt and he came back to his seat with his black shirt on and so I saw that he had another shirt on under his black one and heavy underwear under that. After a few moments, I cleaned my shoes, first with paper and then with the rag you gave me before I left you. After a half an hour, I was ready for a clean collar.

Although I thought of praying when we were lost, I figured that it was a mess for me to get out of and it wouldn't be fair to pass it on to the saints. Perhaps Fr. Metzler prayed. But I did say *Deo Gratias* when I saw the road and when the engineer nodded to me.

Himlerville — Tuesday, June 7, 1927 — 10;30 a.m.

I just mailed my atlas to you, yours will serve my purpose. If at some future time I may wish to delve into European history, I may ask for the use of the volume I am sending you for a year or so.

In the Pennsylvania depot in New York is a large bronze statue of the man who made it possible for the Pennsylvania Railway to get into New York City. Sometimes I feel that I have as big a proposition on my hands in trying to get nuns into Martin County as the unknown gentleman had in getting his depot and railroad into the heart of New York.

My difficulties, I fear, will look small on paper; perhaps they are in reality. Strange to say they are not the difficulties that some other priests have when they wish to open a school. I have plenty of prospective pupils and have been promised all the nuns I need. Moreover, I have the town authorities pulling for me and the promise of some help from the bishop. That certainly looks like easy sailing.

Noonan told me some months ago that two years ago, Himler had offered the county a lot and building if the authorities would establish a high school. Noonan led me to believe that Himler would do the same for me and other considerations led me to the same conclusion. I then wrote to the bishop, stating that I could take care of procuring a school building and asked him if he would allow me $1,000 for equipment and teachers' salary. He said that he would, but was made to understand that that was the limit he would go to. Then comes the decision of the Interstate Commerce Commission allowing the Pennsylvania and Ohio coal fields a twenty cent lower freight rate to the Lake ports, making the differential between those fields and this one 45 cents. The outlook here is poor, On the other hand, at least fifteen Catholic families own their own property. And bad comes to worse. The company will simply go bankrupt and another be organized. However, Himler cannot afford now to be generous. He tried to get a good price for me on a piece of private property; the price asked was too much. He now asks me to build a school, he furnishing the lot and a Sisters' dwelling. I asked him for a six room house which I wanted for both school and dwelling but he says that if we go into cramped quarters, the school will not be received favorably. Moreover, we have enough pupils to get a four year school started this year and Himler says, and rightly, that we must get state recognition or no one will come to the school (at least not those now going to Kermit High School) and that means library and laboratory equipment. To get that all into a dwelling house and make that same house a dwelling for the teachers would injure the plan.

I wired to the bishop Sunday asking him whether I could see him this week. I have no answer yet. He was scheduled for Ashland last Friday and I went there but he wired that he could not come. This is what I want to tell him.

The best chance the diocese has to start something in Eastern Kentucky lies in Himlerville. Fr. Metzler can't do it; Fr. McCrystal can't (i.e. get Sisters in and operate a school); you can't, for one reason that you would have to put on a big front. But I can't finance it. If the diocese would allow me $3,000 instead of $1,000, I believe I could do it because I could take care of the teachers' salary out of my own. I would ask the parish to raise my salary to $100 a month and half of this I would give to the teachers; what the parish couldn't give me (of the $100), I would expect from the diocese. I am afraid the bishop won't allow me any more than he originally promised; I'm afraid he will advise the six room combination idea.

Sisters Vincentia and Domitilla were in Himlerville last Tuesday. Stauncher Catholics kissed their hands; the more timid children spent most of the day under beds. I met them in Ashland Monday night where they were the guests of the Ashland nuns. Tuesday morning they took breakfast in Louisa. They certainly gave Louisa, Ft. Gay and Kermit a thrill! I was very glad to get them back into Ashland late that same night. I was called back to Ashland for a funeral. The poor nuns had to walk quite a bit; our roads are not open yet! Sister Vincentia took three steps on the trestle and couldn't take another unaided. I believe she would have died of fright if a train had come along at the wrong time. An hour ahead of time, we went back to Kermit because the two of them would feel better once they were on the other side of the bridge. When on the other side, we took a ride in Noonan's car and they soon felt better. Mr. Himler received them very nicely, the substance of his talk having been the same as that outlined before.

If the school ever becomes a reality and if the coal company ever gets on its feet, and if and if and if, then perhaps, some day — in a decade of years or so — Martin County may see a hospital, orphanage and old folks' home (all in one) and then some three or four decades later, the church may have made a mark in Martin County. What's 100 years more or less?

Himlerville — Saturday, June 25, 1927 — 11:45 a.m.

I was very blue yesterday for a while, in fact, I was all choked up. I had returned from Covington where I had been told that I was to have no school in Himlerville, made zig-zag connections in order to prolong my stay in Covington and arrived in Kermit at 3:45 a.m. yesterday that I might hear the confessions of and give communion to the couple who were married this morning. The bride did not want to fast too long today, hence the odd arrangements. After coming in at such an hour (4:30), the groom overslept yesterday and so the couple went to Holy Communion at their nuptial Mass anyway. Add to this the fact that I received a long distance call to come to Chateroy, W. Va. for a funeral, Fr. Gleason being in the hospital. The call came too late to make connections in time for the funeral for which I was wanted. Then came a telegram from Fr. Bocklage asking me to come to Ashland today, which would have necessitated my returning at 4:30 a.m. again tomorrow, Sunday. Fr. Bocklage knows I am free on the third and fourth Saturdays and he probably wanted to go to the derby at Latonia. Just before leaving time, another telegram canceled the request of the first one.

I'm feeling all right now after a good night's rest. But, let us record the bitter with the sweet, not exaggerating either, giving a true picture of our disappointments, set-backs and consolations.

Sometime ago I asked for a raise in salary at the time that Hauser, the president, told me that he had asked Kolos, the former president, to give me a Christmas present. About ten days ago, I received a very formal letter with a check for my April and May salary for $50 when it should have been for

February and March. "Please note," ran the letter, "that your suggestion for an increase in salary did not materialize. This is because of our low financial standing at this time. (Signed) G. and R. Catholic Church by William Hauser." The collections have almost doubled in the last three months.

I wrote to the bishop for financial help over a month ago and have no answer yet. A check from a friend of mine came back marked "No funds on hand," and the circumstances are such that all I can do is to try to put the check through again sometime. Fr. Metzler wants to pay his sister back the money she loaned him to come to this country. He wanted to borrow it but I pointed out to him that that would not relieve the situation. So last Wednesday, he and I called on a Mr. Elsaesser, a German, who was recently involved in a million dollar real estate deal and whose daughter, a nun at the Villa I can call a friend of mine, and asked him for help, but we were disappointed.

As for the first disappointment mentioned, the real one, no school — it was a case of: "When you say yes, I may say no." The bishop said: "I am not ready to send nuns to Himlerville,"

And with all this in my head or at least in the background, I flopped into a musty bed at 4:45 yesterday morning, A couple of hours later, when going after a fresh pair of shoes, I found my leather slippers and the straps on my trunk speckled with mildew.

This morning I meditated on Eternity and the whole situation was put into its proper perspective and all these ugly things narrated herein might serve to prepare me for things more ugly.

Himlerville — Saturday, July 16, 1927 — 7:00 p.m.

The last two weeks have been a real vacation for me. The trip to Louisville, on which Dr. Driscoll welcomed us so cordially, and this week's trip to Covington got my mind off local problems.

Last Sunday I tried to make the one o'clock train out of Huntington for Covington to see the end of what turned out to be a most exciting ball game. I went in Schuster's Buick. Five times we pumped up a tire, every five miles, until we finally got to a service station. After we had our tire fixed, we made one more dash to get my train. Then the same tire went down; we had no spare. We fixed it in the hot sun only to find that while fixing the one rear tire, the other one went down, We took turns at getting weak! My hands are still scarred with the blisters of that day.

I tried to work around the chickens for Elizabeth but for two days my hands were no good. Wednesday, four machine loads of picnickers went to Coney Island to witness a real display of fireworks in honor of the Elks whose convention was on in Cincinnati this past week. The display must have cost $5,000. The next thing of this kind will take place on July 4 next year; you must see it! I wanted to witness the affair from the lake and so asked for a canoe. I was told that after eight o'clock, canoes were given to couples only. "Can you get yourself a lady, father?" "I'll be back in a minute," said I and disappeared.

Thursday I was the first to arrive on the scene of an automobile accident and helped to get a man from under his machine. He was bleeding and his shoulder was put out of commission. That night at eleven, I passed Omar Fedders, who while going about forty-five miles an hour, was side-swiped, spun completely around and overturned by someone who is thought to have been a bootlegger and who did not stop. Omar's Ford was demolished. Omar was bruised but did not lose a drop of blood. His buddy found himself in the back seat, whereas he had been located in the front seat. He also was unhurt. The collision took place on a curve.

During the past month, Himlerville celebrated five weddings. No. 1 — two Catholics, at Mass, both received Holy Communion. Ideal. Two days later, he socked her in the jaw because she said if she had known that he had no money, she would not have married him. No. 2 — Mixed, dispensation, in church at 2:00 p.m. No. 3 — Two Catholics, by the squire at Inez, when I was in town. No. 4 — Mixed, by squire. She, 68 years old, was my neighbor. I was in town. No. 5 — Mixed, by minister imported for the occasion, while I was in town.

Today there is a notice on the town bulletin board that from 9:00 to 10;00 tomorrow there will be catechetical instructions for the Catholic children in Hungarian. I'll see to it that the children's Mass won't be out by 9:00 o'clock. I don't know yet what it means. The man who is to give the instructions has been in town only two weeks,

Himlerville — Tuesday, July 26, 1927

I am going to Covington next week and shall send you the copies of American Mercury and Atlantic Monthly that you asked for. Lucy Fedders enters the Benedictine novitiate next week.

I spent a day and a night of last week at Fr. Schulte's mission on Contrary Creek. Catholics have been settled in that territory since before 1800. Those nuns are conducting a summer school for some fifty children, fourteen of whom board at the mission. At Belle Point, the train stops three miles away, is a saw-mill where 75 men are given employment. They work ten and a half hours a day for which they get $2. How can you avoid a "rural problem" under such circumstances? As soon as a man gets sense enough, he goes to Ravenna, a railroad town, or to the "city"! in general. And still, Fr. Schulte says, time and again, they come back to the old log cabin.

I pitched a fourteen inning game yesterday and I'm sore all over today, so sore that I hate to think. I am spending another full week in Himlerville.

In my third letter to the bishop asking for money, I asked for $460 to carry me and Fr. Metzler to the end of the year. I got it by return mail. So it is only fair that I offer you the enclosed check which you so kindly returned to me. If ever I get stuck again, I'll ask you for help.

I forgot to mention before when writing about Belle Point that I narrowly escaped a serious accident when the truck of the locomotive pulling our train, jumped the track while going at top speed. The conductor said that it was luck that kept the locomotive from overturning. I spent a day in Lexington also.

Himlerville — Friday, August 12, 1927 — 1:00 p.m.

During the winter months, I felt that the best season to travel in was the summer. In the beginning of the summer, I concluded that the best time to travel around would be the autumn. But this has been a delightfully cool week and I traveled!

Monday I said Mass at Van Lear at 11:45. In Van Lear I discussed the school situation with Fr. Metzler. But the key-man is now in the Ashland Hospital. That night I took a sleeper out of Ashland for Winchester where I made almost immediate connections for the O & K Junction, one mile from Jackson, where I again made immediate connections for Cannel City where Mike Murphy met me at 1:45 and escorted me to dinner, my breakfast having been two bananas and a Coca Cola. Cannel City is in Morgan County, my territory, but to get to it, I must pass through Fr. Bocklage's. Fr. Bocklage has been there. Bp. Howard, ala Goekel's Ford, passed through the town.

Not far from the city is Cannel coal mine, now over twenty-five years old, employing at this time about sixty men. The coal is loaded into box cars to prevent stealing and sells for $5.50 at the mine. It is a very hard coal that is cut by compressed air machines, and is shipped as far as Boston.

On my return, I missed connections in Winchester by six minutes so I spent the night with Fr. O'Bryan. Next day I motored to Ashland with Frs. Carlon and Jacobs who were passing through Winchester. Our course took us over a nine mile detour, three of which went through a creek. In one place the water was fifteen inches deep. It was while in the creek that Schmitt from Paintsville passed us. He stopped in a shady spot and passed a gallon jug around. Later on we met again in Morehead in a restaurant. After lunch, Schmitt called me aside to tell me that his home was in danger. He had asked his wife and son to accept all of his ready cash and forget him. He has lost his love for his home through his own misconduct and despairs of ever regaining it because of what he has done. However, his wife is taking a sensible stand, simply asking him to go to confession which he is not ready to do, not because he is not repentant but because he is in despair. Our conversation evidently relieved him. He promised to go to confession next week on a trip to Pittsburgh and promised to tell his wife that he was going to go to confession.

The rest of my trip was uneventful except for a noisy blow-out while going at full speed. Fr. Bocklage was, on the surface, in good spirits though a letter from the bishop had been waiting five days for an "answer by return mail."

It is immaterial to you, I suppose, when we go to Mammoth Cave. The latter part of next month would suit me best. I want to visit Logan, W. Va. and the Pike County field. Next week I am going to Warsaw, Ky. for a day to visit Fr. Freiberg and Mary, the occasion being the closing of the Forty Hours Devotion. The week after I want to spend a few days in Covington because of the Villa Madonna festival.

I finished The White Company and enjoyed it. Today I begin the Life of John Marshall by Albert J. Beveridge. Fr. O'Bryan lent me the first volume.

Himlerville — Saturday, August 20, 1927 — 9:00 p.m.

I finished today the first of four volumes of the Life of John Marshall by Albert Beveridge. I learned more history of the United States from this first volume than from any other two historical books put together. I know George Washington better and I had my first encounter with Patrick Henry,

I borrowed the volume from Fr., O'Bryan. If you have not read it, would you want me to send it to you? If I have no answer from you in a week, I shall return it to Fr. O'Bryan and ask him for the other volumes.

Today I went over my library, wiping the mildew off each individual book. I have of late been dreaming of building a rectory in Himlerville rather than of renting a company house because the company is so short of houses. I believe I could build a house in such a way to overcome the mildew pest. But if I do build, I need a housekeeper and the arrangement I now have is so economical. For $15 I get two rooms, heat, light, daily care besides milk and eggs for a month. However, in turn, the oldest girl of the folks upstairs is going to Villa Madonna free of charge. I hope that she will develop into a school teacher for Himlerville. I gave three boys a chance to attend the Latin School, but two turned down my offer and the third could not stand the test I gave him.

Tomorrow I shall administer the last sacrament to a Hungarian who has not been to church for twenty years. Another Hungarian will read the confession and communion prayers to her. There were no natural deaths during my first year in Eastern Kentucky, though five accidental ones.

Himlerville — Thursday, August 25, 1927 — 5:15 p.m.

Last week I spent less than a day in Covington on my way to Warsaw. Monday I went to Huntington to see our sick and then to Covington again, principally because of the Villa Madonna Festival that is to take place Saturday. I feel that I ought to let myself be forgotten in regard to the Villa's annual festival, but I started it some years ago and it took some time to find someone interested enough to take my place. I was in the midst of planning in Covington when a telegram Tuesday night recalled me to Himlerville. So it was duty and not choice that took me from the Festival and I would rather have it that way. I am glad that I was called away.

I wired to Mr. Himler at 6:45 a.m. Wednesday that I was coming. He did not get my telegram until 1:30 and in the meantime, had sent for Fr. Gleason from Williamson who was here when my telegram came and so left again immediately. A three year old girl had died of infantile paralysis. She was buried from the church at 7:30. The coffin was too small for her and a hole was cut at the feet end and the whole thing draped in white. Though no other cases have been reported in Himlerville, children were kept out of the theater and post office and so I followed suit and told them to stay away from church for a while.

Saturday — 12:30

I became so interested in The Spy, by Cooper, that I had to finish that before doing anything else. I spent the morning helping a carpenter making a form for concrete steps to my habitation and also in gathering rock. The vestment case that I asked for months ago was installed about ten days ago.

I shall try your cheesecloth suggestion. I had been studying what to do about it — the mildew — for a week or so and was about to cover the individual books with paper since the mildew seems to effect the leather more than anything else.

Himlerville is a lonesome place but it is no worse than Lynch. Especially now with Veronica gone, it must be more so. My pass enables me to get away. The next time you go to Covington, you might ask for a trip pass and see what happens.

During the past six weeks I have joined in conversation with priests in groups from four to twenty in Lexington, Winchester, Mt. Sterling, Warsaw and Covington. Everywhere was Immaculate Conception Parish the topic of conversation. Fr. Kehoe of Bellevue, 59 years old, wants it bad, so much so that the dopesters give it to him and put Fr. O'Bryan in his place in Bellevue. Fr. Bankemper wants Winchester but the dope boys give it to Fr. McCrystal. It has been said that Nicholasville, Fr. Bankemper's town, was offered to McCrystal with a request to teach in Lexington, but he doesn't want to teach. Schulte and you were discussed over Winchester, but the clergy are under the impression that both of you are willing to wait for your big day, whereas McCrystal is very loud in his desire to get out of Jenkins. How much of this stuff goes to the bishop, I don't know, but he certainly amazed the gang when he sent Geisen to I.C. No one has the slightest notion why this move was made unless it was to stop the talk of what ought to be done or wait until Fr. Kehoe is too old to take it. There is a rumor that the bishop wishes to divide the parish. I feel that you have but a couple of years more of Lynch ahead of you.

Sunday, August 28 — 1:30 p.m.

After a hard day's work, I was asked to take a very sick lady to a Huntington hospital last night.

Mr. Bell doesn't like Catholics. He telephoned from Noonan's house for a doctor for his wife. The doctor said: Hospital. Noonan offered to take Bell and his wife and Bell accepted the generous offer. When Noonan left for the machine, his wife sent for me; she knew Noonan could not be trusted at the wheel. She asked me to go and I said I would and Noonan consented to the arrangement.

We got Mrs. Bell on a chair and Mr. and I carried her down the hillside. Bell is the company electrician. For the first time in his life he addressed a priest with "Father."

It was 7:00 o'clock and I had practically no office said, but I judged that the circumstances were such that I had to proceed on my errand of charity. In Kermit we picked up Dr. Stepp who went along. Twenty miles out, we got a flat. Thirty miles out, the lights suddenly went off and it was the night of the new moon. I found the trouble; luckily it was only a loose fuse. After four hours we arrived at the hospital (68 miles, but much of the road was bad). I took the car to the garage and went to the C & O Depot and said my office. I took a Coca Cola and thirty seconds afterwards, the midnight hour struck. I got the machine, then Dr. Stepp and was at home at 3:30. I don't think Bell will ever speak an unkind word of Catholics again.

Let's get together the week of September 4. I'm ready for Mammoth Cave or Lynch or any other place with you. I could not get to Lexington till

Monday morning. You could spend the night, Sunday, at the hospital but —
"mens sana in sano corpore".

Himlerville — Thursday, September 1, 1927 — 8:00 p.m.

Monday I motored to Williamson and with Fr. Gleason went to Logan, W. Va. where another Jew, Fr. Galegher, is pastor. We went in Noonan's machine, fording a creek fourteen times. We passed through Holden, W. Va. which may be a nicer town than Lynch. At least in Holden there is what I might call a "middle-class." When in their section, one would never think he was in a mining town, with its lawns and hedges and trees.

The Catholics of Logan could be pardoned for being ashamed of their church. The main entrance stands within six-foot of a rock wall. Both Fr. Gleason and Fr. Galegher "have gotten over their zeal." Tuesday we returned to Williamson and I to Himlerville. Wednesday I left for Louisa to break the news to Mrs. Castner that Charles could not hold the pace at the Latin School. In the afternoon, I went to Ashland, returning today over Huntington.

Upon my return I read your last installment. If any change would be welcome, I hope you get Winchester. But we can leave this for oral discussion. I just studied the time table. My meeting you at Norton instead of Jenkins is not practical. I would have to go over Bluefield and would have to spend the night there. So I shall be in Jenkins Monday afternoon. If you think it can be made in a day to the Cave, I'm satisfied. Perhaps we can turn off at Mt. Vernon or Richmond but if we have to go through Lexington and then perhaps through Louisville, it will be a mighty long trip. I did not think Veronica was back in Lynch yet. I'll write to McCrystal; perhaps his going along will determine whether we should go on beyond Lynch or not.

Himlerville — Friday, September 16, 1927 — 3:30 p.m.

Everything was O.K. at Himlerville after our trip through Kentucky, except that two more people were close to death.

Last Monday I left Himlerville at 5:00 a.m. in Schuster's Buick with a Rosie Boza for Villa Madonna. At 5:30 I was leaving Kermit having picked up a Grethel Evans, my first and only convert in this section, also for the Villa, the latter being ready for the fourth year. Through Huntington to Ohio went our course; the roads in Ohio are a dream, straight as an arrow shot for mile after mile, An average of forty miles an hour could be maintained across the state, I believe, without once going over 50. Twice my fan belt came off, the second time probably because I left it too loose the first time. This delayed us because I ran for quite a while at thirty miles trying to bring the thermometer down before looking at the belt, thinking that it was my speeding that heated the motor. We arrived at Elizabeth's about three o'clock.

At five o'clock, I received a telegram asking me to come to Van Lear for a big funeral. I said the Mass for Mrs., McCoart Wednesday and Fr. Metzler played the organ and sang the Requiem. I was called upon for the sake of the sermon. I preached to what seemed like 1,000 people. Pete McCoart said there were over 1,800 people in and around the cemetery. Upon more mature reflection, I believe 400 would be close to it. There were 30 automobiles in front of the church and cemetery. However, nothing like it was ever seen in Van Lear. The McCoart family was one of the first to move into Himlerville 17 years ago.

The next morning Fr. Metzler left for Weeksbury to bury the victim of an automobile accident. The same driver ran off a cliff last summer, incapacitating his wife for months.

Himlerville — September 23, 1927 — 11:30 a.m.

This has been a crowded week. Sunday the married men lost a ball game to the single men, the church benefitting to the extent of $43. I was the umpire. The game was my idea.

Monday noon I arrived in Covington to tend to things left undone there the week before. Tuesday noon I was called back to Himlerville. I drove back in Schuster's machine that I had brought down the week before. A good Catholic had been killed through another's carelessness with a motor. The man died fifteen miles on his way to Huntington. Though married, he did not live with his family; he was a boarder here. So when his coffin came, he was placed in a vacant house. The house was not clean and, except for two candles and two benches made of boards, was empty.

Here I met his daughter and son-in-law.

Wednesday morning I said the funeral Mass though he was not buried till the afternoon because the grave was not ready, When it was too late, the beautiful thought of bringing the casket to church for Mass and leaving it there until burial time came to me.

The daughter carried on according to form. I preached to the largest jam that I ever saw in the Himlerville church. Mr. Villics, the dead man, was the eighth Catholic to die accidentally in my territory. My sermon was an instruction of how to prepare one's self or one's neighbor for death in case a priest cannot be had in time, explaining that "My Jesus Mercy" was the all-sufficient prayer.

At the cemetery, I was ready for trouble. I was tipped off that a Hungarian was going to preach, I made myself Master of Ceremonies, told the men when to rest, the singers when to sing, the men when to let the coffin down and when to close the box. Mr. Fodar, an ex-Catholic and now the self-appointed leader of all the Himlerville non-Catholic Hungarians, did not preach.

As the coffin was brought to the grave, the photographer got busy, The casket was set down and opened and tilted up; the daughter forgot her tears and took her stand on one side and the husband, very seriously, on the other and a picture was taken, Then the wailing was resumed.

That night a Mrs. Glodan died. A boy came in church next morning and told me that a lady had died during the night. I knew who it was, I anointed her ten days ago, though she did not want to receive Holy Communion because she had done so about four months ago. I immediately looked up Mr. Glodan; he was looking for Mr. Himler, I don't know whether he thought of a priest or not. He informed me that his wife's wish was to have a Greek priest for her funeral. I helped him get one. Our first appeal, to the Greek Bishop, was of no avail. Himler then got in touch with Kolos in Cleveland. That night, last night, just after the fight was over and we got the whole thing perfectly at Mr. Himler's residence, Mr. Kolos called from Cleveland saying that he could get a Greek priest provided he was promised $50 and expenses. It is not fit to write what Mr. Himler said but the man is coming. I am to meet him at 3:45 today,

Next day — noon

I met Father Tobacovitch (thus it sounded), at Kermit at 4:15 p.m. and we immediately went to the home from where the funeral was to take place, The ceremony began in the house, was continued in front of the house, then in the side yard where a lengthy sermon was preached. From there we proceeded to the church where I learned that I was expected to preach (it was now becoming dark) and then some more ceremonies on the hill. In the meantime, the church bell was wrung continuously for one hour and twenty minutes — the record up to date, My sermon lasted one minute. At the cemetery, a ten year old daughter of the dead woman was genuinely heartbroken as the coffin went down.

Fr. Tobacovitch looked like a sensible man; I could not believe that he would insist on receiving $50 and expenses. He went to Himler's for supper. I called at 8:30; shortly after a committee called to protest against the priest's demand for $100. Mr. Himler was plainly embarrassed. The committee and the priest went to another room. Their discussion became so loud that we turned on the radio in our parlor. The priest's stand was that he got $35 for such a funeral, that it took two days; that makes $70 and add $30 for expenses. He got it.

At midnight we, the Greek priest, an amicable Hungarian and myself, left in Noonan's machine for Kermit and waited till 1:30 a.m. I got to bed at 2:00.

Himlerville suffered one case of infantile paralysis, fatal, three cases of scarlet fever and an epidemic of mumps this summer. At present, we have no doctor, except one from Kermit.

I may try Covington again next week. If I do, I'll pay Zint and Kuechle!

Himlerville — Saturday, October 22, 1927 — 2:15 p.m.

Again I had completely forgotten about your breviary. I have already written to Kappes and shall now follow the matter up to a settlement.

I have been assigned to inspect Sacred Heart School at Corbin and Mother of God School, Covington. I would like to make Corbin over Lynch but I don't think it would be practical. I am teaching, with help, eighty children on Saturday morning, as I have to be in Himlerville on Friday night. I am also teaching five children in Louisa this Monday afternoon. I would like to get to Lynch some time but not on my Corbin trip because Corbin would take most of the time. Could you meet me on a Tuesday at the top of the hill above Jenkins or would you prefer that we meet in Covington during the Christmas holidays?

As I expected, the feed company asked Joe to return to them though Frank, Joe's father, told Will, who did the firing, that he, Frank, would not ask Joe back as he did once before. This time Will would have to do it. But Will wanted to teach Joe a lesson and wanted Joe to ask for his job. Joe went to the rolling mills but was rejected. Then he was put on at the race track. Just as he was ready to close a deal in Middletown, Ohio, the firm asked him back. All I know subsequent to this is that uncle, who wrote to me, sending me some Masses, has promised Joe security. So he is probably buying a coal and feed business in Middleton — his father going security — but he is so deep in debt that the bank asked for additional security. The business Joe was after sold 160 carloads of coal last year and the price asked for was $15,000. All of which means, I suppose, that Joe and Elizabeth will again sell their home.

Himlerville — Saturday, November 5, 1927 — 9:10 p.m.

It took a half of a week for me to examine the school at Corbin. On my way through Ashland, I picked up a few pamphlets on George Washington to find some material for a lecture for Thursday night. This material made my trip very enjoyable. I took supper in Winchester and left at 10:00 for Corbin. Fr. Placidus had a man waiting for me at the depot after 1:00 a.m. We got to bed at 2:30. I got up at 5:30 to say three Masses at the academy and, after breakfast, did my stuff. Father Placidus and I had dinner at the academy.

I left for Winchester at 3:30 and attended a K.C. social there that night. Next morning I took with me again the first volume of John Marshall's life from which I got my material on roads, drink, illiteracy and — principally — Valley Forge,

I returned Thursday at 4:00 p.m., to learn that an old lady had died that morning. Four Catholics have died this year in Himlerville and no non-Catholics. Next I learned that Schuster had thrown up his job. No doubt you have seen or heard about him in Lynch. That night about forty attended the lecture. I spoke for forty-five minutes — my limit.

Yesterday we had the funeral. Like our weddings, the funerals have become so common that interest has fallen off and this was our tamest.

Today I went into the woods and swung an ax and pushed a saw for a couple of hours and sat before a log fire tonight. For lunch, me and my gang had four pounds of fig Newton's, two pounds of wieners, a peck of apples and a bucket of water.

And now comes the dance — the largest social event of the season! Besides the local orchestra, we shall have a girl orchestra from Covington. Mr. Kuechle will drive the girls to Himlerville.

The date for the dance was first October 23, then November 6, then November 20, and now November 13 because Hauser, the president, is dabbling in Florida real estate and is doing considerable traveling and his schedule was shifting and he had to be here.

I asked the Covington girls to come at a time when I thought Hauser was done with Himlerville. With ladies in the offing, Hauser got busy and made all sorts of plans. One feature was to be a banjo duet by two public school teachers, one a divorcee of 19 winters. These two were summoned to the office a few days ago; it is said that they participated in a game of strip poker with four young men, in which game one's clothes are played for. The boys won no more than the girls' shoes and stockings. Another feature was to be a minuet, a dance between himself and a Grethel Evans, now at Villa Madonna. Hauser proposed that on his next trip to Cincinnati, he take Grethel to a costume establishment, select a costume for her and himself, have a picture taken for purposes of publicity, go to the Villa and practice their dance, etc. I wrote to Sister Vincentia, baldly, and the answer came: Absolutely no! What else Hauser has planned I don't know. He has been gone about ten days and is not due here till November 10 or 11. In the meantime, I'm going ahead along my own lines.

Kappes returned your breviary, having barely touched it up. He says that it would cost almost as much to put it in shape as a new one. It is whole; I can smell "new-skin" on it!! I think I'll send it on to you. I'll be in Covington November 15; if you want me to try Pustet, send the breviary to Covington,

Himlerville Saturday, November 19, 1927 — 11:00 a.m.

It's almost a week since the big dance but it is the first chance I had to write about it.

Hauser left us first and everybody was glad. Four girl musicians came from Covington besides four others, including Sis who had written to me that she was not coming, Adolph Schilmoeller and his wife brought Elizabeth and Mary Agnes in the machine that brought the instruments. They attended Mass at 2:00 a.m. Sunday in Cincinnati and arrived in Himlerville at 1:00 p.m. An hour later came the girls in a Ford driven by Mat Kremer; they had spent the night in Portsmouth.

Noonans took care of two of the girls, the teachers took care of two, Schilmoellers stayed at Schusters and Elizabeth at Bozo's.

The town was waiting for the visitors; the church was fresh in white and green paint. The boys, eight of them, had been practicing vigorously so that they could alternate with the girls in furnishing the music. The dance was not advertised in Kermit but everybody there knew that two orchestras were going to play at Himlerville and one of them was composed of expert girl musicians. I overheard a conversation in Kermit; one man asked another what the admission was going to be. He was told 50 cents; the toll across the bridge was 25 cents, He had 75 cents so he was going,

The girls' first expressions on arriving were of disappointment and disgust and Julia Fedders spoke her mind plainly. "Where's the sense in bringing us to a hole like this?" But that was before she sat down to lunch. When the boys called, the clouds passed away.

The afternoon was spent in getting ready for the evening. A rehearsal with the drum player of the Himlerville orchestra took an hour. The girls did not bring their drums,

At 7:30, the boys opened up with a Hungarian dance. At 7:45, the girls, in new military uniforms, made the hall speechless. The girls played well; their piano player was only 12 years old, And while the boys played, the girls learned to dance the Hungarian dance.

Cake, pie, sandwiches, soft drinks were sold and everything sold had been donated, Because of the poor times, all prices were cut in half and over

$200 were cleared. It was the biggest social event of the season, if not the biggest one in the history of Himlerville.

I learned last night that a blind tiger had been operating under a tree while the dance was going on, Twelve arrests have been made, only two of whom are being held.

We shall have midnight Mass again this Christmas and may keep the Christmas collection, if I can get it.

I left Covington Thursday, Joe said he would settle his problems the next day. He will probably go to Blanchester or Franklin, Ohio. A certain businessman of Cincinnati wanted Joe as a bookkeeper provided he took $2500 worth of stock. But Elizabeth said that she thought Joe would never be satisfied out of the feed business, That is the only expression of opinion that she has so far given, He could, I am sure, establish a successful feed business in Covington; his father would back him, but he refuses to do that.

Himlerville — Monday, December 19, 1927 — 11:15 a.m.

My report for the bishop is almost ready. I am reporting 80 families, 391 souls, 850 Communions, 80 children under instructions, 230 Easter Communions, 65 failing to make their Easter duty, 168 seats in church, 13 members of a Holy Name Society, 100 Catholic children in public school; also 18 baptisms, 7 weddings (two Sanatios), 3 infant deaths and 3 adult deaths (one accidental).

By direction of the Bishop, I appointed next year's officers. I called a meeting of the officers appointed. They were unanimous in their view that they had to be elected. I explained the Church's position; they asked me to nominate a candidate for each office, the people to nominate another. I said I could not. They asked me then to do all the nominating and let the people elect their choice. I said I would submit that idea to the bishop. I did and received no answer, though the matter addressed to him since has been answered. That means I am expected to "stand pat".

The property belongs to the people; legally they must elect trustees for the same. These need not be my committee men but there would be a conflicting of authority if there were two sets of officers. Now that I have begun, I cannot retrace, So I now plan, with the bishop's approval, to call a meeting and ask for the surrender of the property. I can't see myself getting what I want. The alternative will be renting suitable quarters for religious services.

I am leaving for Covington probably on Christmas day. If I or Elizabeth get word that you are coming and if I am in town, I'll meet you at the depot.

I'm sending you a $2 gift in appreciation for your exertions in getting me to Jenkins.

Himlerville — Sunday, January 1, 1928 — 9:30 p.m.

A meeting of the Catholics was called while I was out of town and a set of officers was elected in spite of the fact that I had appointed a set. A friend wrote to me about it and I laid the whole matter before the bishop. He shrugged his shoulders and said: "I guess all we can do about it is to pray." I asked the men elected to meet once a month in my quarters hoping to gain a stronger hold. They met here this afternoon and agreed to settle everything by a majority vote. My salary was raised from $25 to $40 a month. In other words, the church now pays my rent over and above my $25 salary. I was then asked to itemize the things that Kolos gave me when he left Himlerville, they being the property of the church, so they said. When I got to the bed, they wanted to know what went with the bed; how many blankets, etc. This was all put into the minutes. Nothing else was settled; the meeting lasted over two hours.

Enough events have taken place during the last ten days to fill twenty pages of diary but my mind is tired. I write this tonight because tomorrow I pull out again for Louisa and Van Lear and Ashland. I am going to Van Lear principally because of the annual report, Metzler asked me to be there when it comes to filling it up for the Bishop,

I had a full week in Covington last week, arriving on Christmas day itself and staying until Saturday morning. Wednesday I went to Franklin to see Joe's place. I think he has a wonderful opportunity. We received your account of your Christmas; Schuster wrote that you had reason to be glad on Christmas.

Himlerville — Friday January 27, 1928 — 8:00 p.m.

In your last installment you write that you waited for news more interesting or more disgusting, and I felt that you were waiting but I hated to think of the effort required to outline details of a situation that is forever changing. It was all so novel once, but now — you know how it goes. Once there was a time when a trouble was settled, I fondly hoped that all trouble was settled; now I merely wonder in what shape it will reappear.

Because of your kindly interest, I shall go into the matter a little more exhaustively. My appointments were politic. I appointed Fekete president, Gurdon vice-president. Next day, Gurdon passed me on the street. "How are you," said I. "No good. How did you sleep," said he. "Fine. How did you sleep?" "No good, awake all night. You like Fekete better than me," and so Gurdon went from house to house knocking Fekete and proclaiming his platform for when he will be elected president. His platform was: a fence around the church, a statue of St. Stephen in the church, clearing up of the debt and raising the pastor's salary. He, himself, called the meeting and was elected president by a majority of three votes, Seven officers were elected, four of them Greek. I never saw the vice-president in church until he was elected.

The meeting that elected Gurdon, however, curtailed his authority. Up until then the president was 99% of the board and Gurdon expected to be 100% of the board. The meeting voted that the president could act only with the approval of the majority and the majority is Greek! So Gurdon then came to me and suggested that he and I ignore that dictum of the meeting and run the parish to suit ourselves! But I am surer of getting a majority of the board in my favor than I am of getting Gurdon, so I won't buck the majority.

However, the whole crew is now reckoning without me. We have but $250 debt left (it was $900 a year ago) and it seems that when the debt is paid, that the coal company wants to give someone a deed to the property. The Greeks have requested Mr. Himler *not* to give it to the Roman Bishop and the Romans have requested him *not* to give it to the Greek Bishop. The reason I underscore the negative is that each side is more concerned about their opponents gaining a victory than they, themselves, are about suffering a loss. So at this time, "trouble" takes the form of a war between the Greeks and the Romans. And strange to say, I don't give a rap who gets the deed! I have not analyzed my feelings. I know I won't get it just because I want it and if I do get it, I know that that won't end Mr. Himler's trouble. Perhaps I have lost gumption; I don't know. All I say to myself is: none of this is vital to religion.; if I fight, it may end my career here; if I let it alone, I can at least continue instructing the children and strengthening them in their faith.

With it all, attendance at Sunday Mass never was better. I now have the children at their own Mass, praying in common and singing and every seat is taken at the second Mass. In fact, so lustily are we singing that the Presbyterians have in true Protestant fashion reorganized and are now conducting a Sunday school in the school building, a Reverend from Inez riding over on his horse every Sunday.

Since I left Van Lear, the Consolidation has changed the management there. The only one I know well, and that through Metzler, is Pfender who is in charge of all machinery, so I think Mr. Hahn is your best bet though Fr. McCrystal might be able to make a good connection for you.

I was in Covington last week to take a sick lady to the hospital. I was there this week to get out St. John's report. I have been asked to speak at the nurses' graduation in Covington next week and the following week I promised Lucy Fedders to come to Covington on the occasion of her reception into the Benedictine Order, Last week I outlined for uncle just what had to be done in getting out the report, So little confidence has he in his assistants since I left that he brought the work over to the Sisters. It took four of them a whole day to do what Fr. Egbring and a kid or two could have done in half a day. The Easter collection envelopes were not yet in alphabetical order last week!

And some more trips to Covington are looming. Instead of allowing an appropriation for Van Lear and Himlerville, I have been asked to try first to raise the money I need along the lines that Fr. Carlin plans, as outlined in today's Catholic Telegraph. I am now arranging to have the dramatic club from Latonia give a play for us in the Covington library auditorium, if possible, before Lent. I'll be very glad to see your new church but let's make no plans now because the next month or so is so uncertain for me.

Himlerville — Saturday, February 4, 1928 — 9:00 p.m.

When Gurdon called the meeting during Christmas week that elected him president, Kolos was in town. I knew the meeting was called and I confided in Kolos and asked him to fight for me. He wrote to me afterwards saying everything turned out lovely and then proceeded to tell me who was elected! (He wrote to me while I was in Covington,) I thought he double crossed me. I told the bishop the whole affair and was called down for trusting Kolos whom the bishop regards as a traitor.

A week ago tonight, Kolos mysteriously dropped into town, ostensibly to visit his lady friend. But three times in two days, I found him and our president together. Monday I went out on the same train with him and from him I learned the following: that the meeting that elected Gurdon president did not decide that he had to abide by the decision of the majority of the officers but it decided that he, Gurdon, could not act without my approval. Kolos then told me why he had been sent for. When I left town at Christmas time, the Greek priest hung around for two or three days, Upon his arrival, he acknowledged me as pastor and explicitly asked me for faculties and authorization to act in my name. When I left, he called the Greeks together and explained to them that he did not come under the jurisdiction of the Latin bishop and whether Bishop Howard liked it or not, he could come any time and say Mass. And since theirs was a Roman and Greek church, why not have Mass in the Roman rite one Sunday and in the Greek rite the next Sunday? And since the Greek rite priests were Hungarian, why not induce Mr. Himler to give the Greek Bishop a deed to the church property? No one told me of this how-de-do, not even the president who wanted to run the parish in partnership with me! Instead, he writes to Cleveland, Kolos comes down and soft-soaps the Greeks, and writes to their priest to keep out of Himlerville and is good enough to tell me all about it.

These are some of my reflections: Himler may not give Bishop Howard a deed, but he is too honest to give it to the Greek Bishop. I am despairing of ever obtaining pastoral relations over these people, but my plan is, as soon as the opportunity presents itself, to run for president myself and once elected, to arrange that the pastor, ex-officio — is president. If defeated, I move.

An old lady died Sunday. I went for a boy to toll the church bell. At the boy's home, I found Gurdon, the president, & Kolos, I sent the boy down the road instructing him not to ring the bell like at a wedding but to toll it and while he was gone, I talked to Gurdon and Kolos. Presently I heard the bell, wedding fashion. Upon the boy's return, I asked for an explanation and he told me that as he began to toll, one of the officers, Kish, told him to ring it otherwise. Upon being told that Fr. Hanses did not want it that way, the boy was told: "Fr. Hanses ain't boss around here." Thereupon Gurdon rose and went down the road to make sure that Kish knew who was boss! Kish is a Greek and up until Christmas was very friendly to me, telling me then that when his hogs were killed, he wanted me for dinner some time. His hogs are now killed but the invitation to dinner has been forgotten.

Himlerville — Saturday, March 3, 1928 — noon

Father Danz is now Assistant at St. Aloysius so I think he is out of the question and I don't know whether he can speak Polish. Nor do I know of any in our diocese who do. You might be able to get a Franciscan.

Father Metzler has been told that he may stay where he is until he finds another bishop, his record being such that he, the bishop, could give him a favorable letter. I felt this almost as keenly as Father Metzler. What is actuating the bishop we don't know. It may be one of two things: he may want to get me out of Himlerville, not satisfied with the course of events here; he may be thinking of the five men to be ordained in June. I shall see the bishop Wednesday. I am not expecting a pleasant interview. Nothing seems to be pleasing him. Carlin, whom I visited for a night, refuses to pay his diocesan assessment; Bocklage is having his troubles with him. I had to pay 3% assessment on $650 the Hungarians paid on their church debt. The bishop is waiting for me to put something on for the missions. He promised the Daughters of Isabella to let them put on a $1,000 affair for the missions. I want to hook up with them but that's too easy. Father Reiter will let me use his dramatic club but I must play in a Catholic Hall. Father Tappert will let me have his auditorium but the cast must not be mixed, Father Reiter, on principle, won't "unmix" his cast.

Sunday — 10:15 p.m.

I had a lot more to say but was called away, Father Francis of Gary is probably Polish; would you like to exchange pulpits with him for a Sunday? You may send me your oil stocks in care of uncle.

Himlerville — Monday, March 19, 1928 — 11:00 a.m.

I must unsay some of the things I recorded last time. The bishop told me that he had not meant to drop Father Metzler but simply would not incarnate him and he wished I would impress it strongly upon Father Metzler that he hoped he would not leave the diocese. I have learned since that two others have received similar notice, who have been given places as "guests."

The bishop has also given me full charge of the Daughters of Isabella social. I get the entire proceeds, I got this concession only after I suggested that I could bear some of the expense of schooling two boys I am preparing for the Latin School.

I am at present deep in Himlerville politics and it is a thrill to know some things that the other fellow doesn't think you know. The Greeks had a contract drawn up which would have bound the signers not to attempt to surrender the church property to any party and to forfeit all their rights in the property if they attempted to do so. The Greeks do not know that I have a copy of this document. Two of the Romans are afraid that the Greeks might push this thing, so we have decided to call for a show-down. Next Sunday is the last Sunday of the 52 for which I gave out weekly envelopes last year; so Sunday morning I plan to read off the names and amounts contributed during the past year and call a meeting of all of those whose names were read off for the afternoon. This will eliminate three of the twelve Greeks. At this meeting, I'll distribute the next season's envelopes and then ask them to sign a contract surrendering all their temporal rights to Bishop Howard. Some of the Greeks may quit church, but I am confident that a sufficient number of the "owners" of the church property will sign the paper to warrant me to proceed to make legal claim to it. Another of the Greeks will be on the ocean Sunday. To another I have offered the opportunity to send his girl to Cardome next year at the diocesan expense; I am helping still another to locate a business. The contract I shall lay before them gives the Bishop their title to the property on three conditions acceptable to Bishop Howard, namely: (1) that Bishop Howard sends a Hungarian priest to Himlerville from time to time; (2) that the Hungarians be permitted to continue to sing in Hungarian; (3) that the salary of the pastor is not to exceed in dollars per month the number of Catholic families.

This is going to be a "kill or cure" proposition. Though I have not discussed this part of the subject with the Bishop, if I lose, I intend to let the people know that it will be a matter only of a few weeks and I'll be gone and the next priest will come in on Bishop Howard's terms,

Himlerville worked three days last week. That's the best for some months. It looks like four days a week next month. We had a St. Patrick's Day celebration for the benefit of the striking miners. I was the first speaker; net receipts $58. The only Irishman in Himlerville went to a dance in Huntington that night. Except for my talk and some Irish songs, the whole verbal program was in Hungarian.

Tonight I'll be in Williamson, Tuesday in Louisa, Wednesday in Ashland, Thursday in Van Lear, and Friday home. Next week I expect to spend here.

Himlerville — Thursday, March 29, 1928 — 9:30 a.m.

Kolos was Himlerville's Pope Leo; Hauser, his successor, was Wilhelm der Grosse, and Gurdon, the present boss, is Charlie the lion-hearted because Francis I, the leader of the Greeks, and the church treasurer, can't make Charlie budge. Kolos is in Cleveland, Hauser in Florida and forces in Cleveland are pulling things my way and forces in Florida are trying to disrupt the peace that has been existing in the Catholic part of Himlerville.

Himler, I believe, is carrying water on both shoulders. His coal company is regarded by coal operators as an outlaw company. He would not join their association; his was to be an independent company; he was going to pay the wages he wanted and so on. I think he feels the same about the church; an independent church is his ideal. Rather than have him hear from others what I was about to do, I went directly to him and told him that since Bishop Howard would not make the promises I asked him to make upon which he would be given a deed to the church property, I was going to ask the people to sign a contract, giving the Bishop their title to the property, as far as it went, on certain conditions. These conditions are three: that the Bishop will provide a Greek priest from time to time; that he will not interfere with the Hungarian language; and that the pastor's salary was never to exceed in dollars per month the number of Catholic families. I submitted my whole proposition to Bishop Howard and got no answer though he told me he would answer by March 25. I went ahead and the Bishop can accept or reject the title as he pleases.

Mr. Himler said that he would be glad if I could put an end to church fights and elections but I should pacify the Greeks first. I met six Greeks Saturday night. Three of these I had befriended in various ways. I explained what I wanted: all I wanted was that I should be boss, I should appoint my officers, I should sign all checks. They came back with: if the Bishop gets what he wants, he will take me away and send them a man like Father Whalen! "No, please, leave the church independent; why cause a lot of trouble."

I called a meeting Sunday afternoon. Almost everybody was there. Sentence for sentence my talk was translated into Hungarian. I told them that I would visit them individually and ask them to sign the contract that I explained to them. But this is what hurt the Greeks: the last of the envelopes I gave out a year ago was dropped in the basket that morning. I read a report of the envelope contributions. One Greek gave 25 cents, another 80 cents, a third $1.75, two gave nothing and altogether they gave less than the parish gave a Greek priest to come to Himlerville on Christmas day to say one Mass after I had said the midnight Mass and children's Mass, followed by my third. Father Dzuboy, the Greek priest, got $75, The Greeks demanded that their contract be read at the meeting also, a contract that Mauser, a Roman, had paid $15 to have drawn up by an attorney to "fix it" that Bishop Howard would never get title to the property. I don't know why Hauser never asked anyone to sign this contract which stated that anyone who attempted to surrender his title to the church property to any party forfeited his title! When this bastard was read, the Greeks brightened up, nodding their heads in approval.

Now comes in another detail. Lovass, our postmaster, about twenty-five or thirty years old, asked me for a box of envelopes about a half a year ago. In fact, Hauser asked me for Lovass. Lovass was in church once and contributed $1.00. He was getting ready to succeed Hauser as president and he knew about Hauser's contract. Lovass is also Roman. But Lovass never became president because I surprised him by appointing the officers and though my appointments were set aside, he was not enough of a church member to lead the fight against my appointments. I told the Greeks Saturday night that I was going to read the names and amounts of the envelope contributors Sunday afternoon. Lovass was not in church Sunday, but Monday in entering the contributions of the day before, I saw that Lovass donated $2. However, Sunday's contributions were not included in my report Sunday afternoon and so I read: "Mr. Lovass — $1.00." Mr. Lovass was there. I was told that he came as Himler's spokesman. Himler calls Lovass crazy and a nut but I believe this is a blind. But I didn't give Lovass a chance to speak. I said what he had come to say; I said that I knew that I could not get a deed to the property, i.e. the ground, because Mr. Himler informed me that the owner had died and the law of Kentucky says that miners cannot dispose of inherited property. All I wanted, I said, was whatever title the people had. Frankly, I am afraid Himler is tricking me but please don't say that I said this; I intend to investigate,

I called the meeting closed and Lovass started: the people can't give the Bishop a deed; nobody can get a deed and so on. Things got so hot, I put everybody out of the school building.

Monday the mine worked. Tuesday I started out with an interpreter. The opposition of the Greeks united the Romans and so far, only one out of the first thirty-three heads of families I approached has refused to sign my contract and he won't sign because he got stuck once when he went on another fellow's note. Moreover, two Greeks have signed and some more want to sign.

Gurdon, the president, is all for me. Frank Kish is the leader of the Greeks. Kish handed Gurdon Hauser's contract to take action on it and Gurdon "lost" it! Kish had Gurdon summoned before the Police Judge yesterday (Noonan is P.J.) to surrender the document that Hauser had given him, Kish. Noonan asked who the owner was. Kish said Hauser paid $15 for it and sent it to him. Noonan said: Send it back to Hauser; then Gurdon produced it!

I have not asked Noonan to sign so as not to embarrass him before Mr. Himler who says that the whole thing is a fight between Kish and Gurdon, Greek and Roman, and no one knows what he is signing. Noonan asked me last night to drop the matter (he said he was speaking for Mr. Himler) and collect no more signatures. I'll stop when I get forty, a safe majority. Though I'll go easy, I'll appoint the same officers who are now in office, even Frank Kish. I'll let Kish sign the checks after I sign them; I'll let him keep the bank book and deposit the money, At the end of the year, he automatically goes out of office with Gurdon and I'll appoint two new ones.

If you don't mind, please let Schuster read this because he would enjoy it. No; don't. I said too much about Himler.

Himlerville — Monday, April 23, 1928 — 10:00 a.m.

I obtained 40 signatures to the contract giving the Bishop title to the church property here. I could get more. I shall continue to gather signatures as chance directs one or the other Hungarians to my room. Three of the forty signers have already moved from Himlerville.

I am now being boss on paper. I asked my friend, the Roman leader, to turn over the bank book, check book and cash book. But nothing doing! He was not surrendering anything until *he* had everything fixed up. He wants an iron fence around the church, a choir loft in it and the debt canceled and then he doesn't care what happens! He was just in my room; he was mad at me since 11:00 a.m. yesterday, said he. He threatened to resign, call a meeting and have a successor appointed (!) and did not care what happened to the Catholics of Himlerville. And all this because of two things: one a misunderstanding that I cleared up by drawing a picture and the other because I had spoken a conciliatory word to a couple of Greeks who gave in to Gurdon, my Roman leader friend, on the very thing he wanted.

In your last installment, you expressed the opinion that perhaps all this fuss was not worth the little good it was producing. I, too, for a long time, felt that the good I was slowly building up could totter and then crash in a day. But this is a small town, a very small "small town" and one man's quarrel is often taken up by the whole town. Most of the stuff I have been recording about the Greek and Roman War is smoke but with it all, I am gaining; I am slowly but continually strengthening my hold. I'll appoint my own officers henceforth; in that I am determined even if I have to take up the collection myself at Sunday Mass in case no one accepts my appointment which I do not expect, I'll announce all diocesan collections after this and get them. The iron fence is just what I want that I can determine definite limits to the property and Himler has told Gurdon how far he has to stay away from the bank building in setting up a fence around the church. The choir loft is not a bad idea either because we need room.

It looks like a lot of trouble but no harm that I can see has been done to religion and these folks must have something to fuss about. I realize, however, that it may take several years to educate the people to think the way I do and I am sure that if the Bishop made a change here now, it would take my successor a long time to get to where I am now. I am an old-timer in Himlerville. There was a time since I am here that six and even eight families were waiting for a house in Himlerville; now plenty are empty, with plenty more housing families whose heads have gone to the city to work. Those who have come to Himlerville since I have, never think of crossing me.

I have not heard yet what my social in Covington netted but I hope it will be about $800. The afternoons were poorly attended but there were good crowds in the evenings. If the D of I repeat this social next year, I hope they will make it 50 cents a tally in the afternoon and $1 in the evening instead of $1 all around as this affair was,

Himlerville — Friday, July 27, 1928 — 8:15 p.m.

The cup of misery seems full. A touch of gloom overshadowed Himlerville when work fell to two days a week. The limit was reached, it was thought, when work dropped to two days, but even then there was the assurance that in April, the mine would work full time. In the beginning of April, the railroads of the Ohio-Pennsylvania field met with the railroads of the West Virginia- Kentucky field to prevent a rate war. The meeting broke up in disharmony. Later an agreement was reached: a 35 cents differential in freight rates favoring Ohio & Pennsylvania was agreed on. As a consequence, Himlerville got no Lake Coal and we are still working but two days a week. In the beginning of May, the Receivers did not have enough money to meet the payroll; this caused a rush on the bank which promptly collapsed. The miners have been working since to give them credit in the store which, in turn, is holding on, solely because of the generosity of the multi-millionaire Receiver, Mr. Hatton. Then, four weeks ago, came the flood. It is only two and a half miles to the head of the creek that caused the trouble. How so much water could collect in that distance is almost unbelievable. Sixteen houses were swept off their foundations, fifteen of them being heaped up together against a two story house that held, inflicting considerable damage to it. And the fifteen houses still lay where the water left them; the creek is still full of silt. The Red Cross, which looked the place over, has not even sent us lime. What the town would have done without Bishop Howard's $2000, I don't know. I have given out over $1,750 for all sorts of purposes — from bringing babies into the world to burying the old folks!

And the end is not yet. The mine is for sale, at auction, as you know, on August 10. Several big companies have been looking the place over and everybody is hoping that there will be a buyer. Everybody is owing everybody else and if the credit chain breaks, there will be untold misery. Is it as bad as this, or perhaps worse, in Pennsylvania, I wonder.

The Bishop promised to pay for two girls at Cardome and two boys at the Latin School. Conditions are such that I don't think a single one will be able to accept the opportunity. Instead, I plan to place the girls in Ashland homes where they can work for their board and perhaps a few dollars, and attend the high school there, The boys, I suppose, will go into the seventh grade here.

Last Tuesday I spent the day with the boys. Because of the hard times, I asked the boys to bring only bread with them and I would supply the rest. Besides bread, they brought green apples and green peaches and onions. Mrs. Noonan baked a supply of cookies and I provided dogs, crackers and so on, This, together with blankets, hatchets and nine buckets of drinking water, constituted our supplies. The hatchets were to supply a shelter for the night, but we gave up the idea of a shelter. Twenty-two of us slept under the stars that night. The girls became so envious that they prevailed on Mr. & Mrs. Noonan to take them last night. At 2:00 a.m., the rain drove them home! But I believe they were glad to be driven home.

Editor's Note (from *History of the Diocese of Covington, Kentucky*)

Himlerville, a coal camp, also known as *Beauty*, is located among the mountains in the eastern part of Martin County. During the boom days, the Catholic population increased to more than five hundred. From 1926 to

1928, Rev. Henry Hanses served as resident pastor at St. Stephen Mission. When the Himler Coal Company failed in 1928, many of the Catholics left the community.

Father Henry then became pastor of The Church of the Resurrection at Lynch, Ky. replacing his brother, Father Alfred. He remained there until 1945 when he returned to St. John's in Covington.

PRIVATE DIARY

Beginning at the opening of a diocesan retreat
at Gethsemani, Kentucky
November 9 1936

TRAPPIST MONASTERY — Thursday, November 9, 1936 — 8.15 a.m.

Father Spain and I were the last to arrive last night after 240 miles of driving, though Father Spain had already driven 120 miles before I met him in Cumberland.

We were well received, of course, though we had a hard time finding the bell rope in the dark.

I was one of the first in the Library this morning for meditation. I sat there and studied the priests as they came in. A bunch of saps was my first impression, the longer in the priesthood, the fatter they get; perfectly fitting cassock, some nice warm cloaks; smug, comfortable, plenty of money. Last night we pulled up along side of a Packard.

Saps! And I came to Gethsemani in a new overcoat and though my car is not two years old, I will have a new one before the end of the month; a coupe with the spare tire just where I want it, a turret top that will never leak, a grill that won't come loose, running boards unattached to the fender, a windshield defroster and a heater. Saps!

I looked around, Couldn't I find anything to edify me? The young priests weren't so fat. The retreat Master, an old man, was kneeling on the floor unsupported. Just showing off! No, the bishop could think what he pleased but the retreat Master would simply be himself. The simplest man in the meditation room, aside from the retreat Master, was the Bishop, and the only Monsignor present, Msgr. Woeste, was not showing off either. It was proper for him to wear his special cassock. He would prefer to wear the ordinary priest's cassock, that is why the Monsignorship suits him. There is nothing pompous put on about Bishop Howard and skinny Monsignor.

My first impulse at this retreat is to go on a diet — I weigh 206 — and to wear out my new clothes and new car as soon as possible.

8:45 p.m.

The substance of the first Conference was that I have a very definite destiny in this life, of the second, that without God, I can do nothing, of the third, that there must be conformity between God's Will and mine. The most impressive thing taken from the reading during meals was that a priest looks better to his flock from the distance. I must withdraw more from my congregation. RESOLVED: not to go to Johnson's for supper every Sunday and to arrange, at my convenience, to get away from taking my meals at Mr. McCarthy's.

I noticed that the heels on the retreat Master's shoes were cut out of an old tire and that his conference notes were written on scratch paper — and that the brothers were operating a new Dodge truck, which may prove that the vow of poverty may be served best by spending money in the proper way.

Perhaps I can convince others that a new car is an economy. Here are several tables of figures showing that my present Dodge costs less to operate than my former Pontiac, a second hand car.

	Pontiac(old)		Dodge(new)	
Monthes used	24		21	
Miles travled	22,000		27,000	
Daily average miles	30		42	
Cost, perday	$1.12		$1.50	
Cost, permile	.0375cents		.035cents	
	Amount	Rate	Amount	Rate
Gas	390	.45	395	.395
*Depreciation	390	.47	395	.263
Repairs, Tires, Ins.	200	2.41	250	.165
Oil, Grease, Cleaning	125	.151	100	.105
Garage, Parking, etc.	70	.084	60	.063
License	15	.018	15	.016
Interest on invest.	30	.036	50	.053
Totals	830	1.00	950	1.00

(*)The difference between the price paid for car and received for car.

GETHSEMANI-Tuesday, November 10, 1936 -5:45p.m.

The retreat Master is very dry, but that makes no difference. His principles are fundamental and a priest needs only to come into contact with them regularly and the more unadorned the better. The gist of today's conference was simply to order one's day and to work in a spirit of humility and obedience.

I made my confession this afternoon and the retreat is worth the biennial review of one's life since the last retreat. My confessor asked me how long I took to say Mass, then he told me that I did not give the Holy Ghost a chance! I have promised to make a weekly hour of adoration to review the lessons of this retreat, until my next retreat. My feet are too cold, I can't think.

GETHSEMANI -Wednesday, November 11, 1936 — 1:30 p,m.

I have averaged one hour of Adoration per week since the beginning of my theology course, over twenty years ago, which, by the way, puts me across the 1,000 mark. Since 1925, I have made a vow every year to make a weekly hour of adoration. I have just renewed that vow for another year.

As I leave Gethsemani, it is my resolution, my hope and my prayer — and I got this idea at the Sixth Station a little while ago — to be nothing from now on but a priest, to be nothing in Lynch but a priest, to be nothing to Mary Agnes, to the Johnsons, to the McCarthys, to the Mecicas, but a priest.

I have forgotten mortification. I resolve to give up smoking for the rest of my life.

I have just finished the life of Bishop Chaloner of London in the days of the American Revolution.

LYNCH, KY. Friday, March 20, 1937 — 9:30 p.m.

Just returned to Lynch from Sis' Funeral. I have no more a place that I can call home.

Daniel Paul was born on January 28th; I saw Elizabeth the next day, evidently happy and apparently well. On February 24th, as I was preparing to leave Covington for Lynch without having called up Elizabeth, I received a call from her, she having learned that I was in Covington while attempting to get me in Lynch, I wired to Lynch, canceling the Lenten Services scheduled for that evening, and hurried to Franklin. I found her depressed and very sick. I left that night, promising to return in a week or ten days. Sunday night Joe called for me in Lynch and the police did not locate me until they had awakened several families looking for me. Because of deep snow, I did not leave until next morning and then drove all the way to Franklin, arriving in the early evening.

Sis was very sick, rheumatism of the heart muscles. The nights were so long; she could not lie down; had not been on her back for 2 or 3 weeks; her legs were swollen; asthma bothered her severely; the baby was back in the hospital; I was up a dozen times the first night with Alfred suffering from asthma, Mary Agnes was sick in another room with influenza, On the next morning, Joe and I were up with Sis, crying nervously, begging us to do something for her. We prayed the rosary.

That day, Tuesday, March 2, I went to Dayton and bought a back rest. It helped her a little. We took Alfred to a child specialist after he coughed an hour and a half with every breath, Mary Agnes was better. Sis felt better — until the long night once more frightened her. Wednesday morning I took her out for a short ride; she enjoyed it. That afternoon we took a longer ride. That night I left. Next day, her mother-in-law came out and spent a few days with her.

I did not go up to Franklin the week of March 7. I called frequently. Once she got three hours sleep. Saturday, March 13, I was told she was no good, I went back to Franklin the next day. I started out to Franklin but Omer met me in Covington and told me that Sis was back in the Middletown Hospital under an oxygen tent, and I realized that the last chapter was being written, When we got to the hospital, she was sleeping. In an hour, she was awake. Upon seeing me, she said: Up all day and all night? For the next forty hours, I was in and out of her room continually telling her a hundred times that I was so glad to be with her, After Mass I anointed her. As I reached for her eyes, I lost control of my emotions, knelt down and let the tears roll. She put her hand out from inside the cellophane tent, took my hand and said: "I'm going to pull through, Henry, honest I am." Never once until the end did she whimper, I proceeded with the anointing. Not a word did I say in English, thinking only of the verbal integrity of the prayers I was reading.

Uncle was to come on the 11:00 o'clock traction, He missed it and so I gave Sis the Viaticum. Uncle arrived at one and remained an hour. He was very kind. Alfred arrived at 3:00 o'clock and first satisfied himself, by going to Dr. Gerber"s office, that there was nothing more to be done physically for Sis. Alfred stayed up all night, I slept from 11:00 to 3:00; Joe slept from 4 to 7. Mary Agnes and Francis came in the beginning of the morning and Sis most touchingly bade them good-bye, Mary Agnes promising her to love your girl and to take good care of her three little brothers,

Her troubles became severely acute shortly after I returned after my sleep. Her pain was terrific at times, "My God, why can't I die?" From her breast down, she was swollen, A toties quoties crucifix was resting on her abdomen in such a way that she could easily study the sufferings of Our Lord. "O God, if I have offended You, I'm sorry; if I have done anything, anything." "Holy Mary, Mother of God, pray for us sinners now and at the hour of our death." Later: "My Jesus mercy." Also "Into Thy hands I commend my spirit." All this without prompting. She turned to me and Joe: "Can't you do something?" And I answered: "Sis, you are being crucified just a little bit longer. Mother is waiting for you, Daddy is waiting for you, and Joe and I will be coming soon. You will get things ready for us, won't you?" And she answered: "But the children." I then told her: "Sis, you can do more good for Mary Agnes in heaven than you could here on earth, Mother took care of you from heaven, didn't she?" This seemed to satisfy her,

It was after 1:00 o'clock in the afternoon when I went out for some breakfast — a half plate of soup. A minute after I returned, about two o'clock, her agony ended with Joe and Alfred and I and a Miss Hombert around her. We all knelt down and said a few prayers.

Now she rests next to Mother in St. John's Cemetery and I fear death less than I ever did before.

As Joe and I got into the car to return home, he said: "Now I have no one left but you." There was no sense to his remark but who could say anything sensible under the circumstances? At home, Joe called Omer and simply said: "I'm home."

TRAPPIST MONASTERY, Thursday, November 9, 1937 — 1:00 p.m.

This year's retreat began after supper last night. I was the first to arrive in the middle of the afternoon. I was shown to my room; went to the window, opened it, looked out on a monastery garden as a monastery bell rang out, in a drizzle of rain. And I thought: This is living! If only Harry Moses and his wife could come here for a week, I attended an Armistice Day banquet in Lynch last Saturday night at which Harry Moses presided. The dinner was not so bad but after it was served, Mr. Moses hooked his arm into mine and took me to his room. There I had to listen to lewd songs and the dirtiest stories I have ever heard in my life, Harv and Ann Johnson came in; and within a minute they found an excuse to get out. It would serve no purpose to describe this party in detail, it left two impressions on me: I came out of that room with a deeper respect for Lynch ladies for they maintained their dignity in the presence of visiting ladies who did not, and "hunky" christenings and weddings went up in respectability by comparison with what I witnessed in the Big Shot's room who, I was told, later took it upon himself to kiss many of the ladies good night!

I was sorry for Harry Moses as I looked out of my monastery window. And I was blue for Sis. There is no one who will miss me like I miss Sis. It is not necessary for someone to miss me. It means nothing to Elizabeth that I miss her; praying for her perhaps does mean something to her. I wonder sometimes if Joe gets as blue for Sis as I do. I suppose he does. Omer tells me that he looks at the newspaper thirty minutes at a time without turning a page. Joe himself tells me that his greatest anxiety is that his children may grow up friendless, and therefore he is both father and mother. I would like to see the children show their pain of loss a little but that may come later when they are older and Joe or I can talk to them about their mother.

My most prized possession, next to my faith and my vocation, is the memory of Sis. I call her Sis because she never was Betty to me. Perhaps I felt much the same when mother died fifteen years ago; namely, that the memory of her was such a treasure to me. I recall positively that it was. Time has, of course, faded that memory. I recall how I visited mother's grave every Sunday evening for several years, often foregoing supper. I have much reason to be proud of mother and I am just as proud of Sis. Mother died a natural death, Sis died of unselfishness. But there is no need of making comparisons. Right now I am blue for Sis and I am not ashamed of it.

While I was standing at my window, Father Poole, the second arrival, stepped into my room and his first word after our mutual greeting was about Sis' death. The last time we had met was when I was on the way to see Sis last January, just as Paul Daniel was born.

Our retreat this year will last only three days and four nights. That gave me one day for daddy, one day for mother, and one day for Sis. I have already made one hour's adoration for dad and I have time for another before the day is over. I'll say the rosary before the Blessed Sacrament for him and the Way of the Cross, I don't know how many indulgences that means for him but since he only needs one, we need not take time counting up all the indulgences I can gain. Tomorrow will go to mother's account and Thursday's share will be for Sis.

The conferences so far have been very simple — the length of eternity, the certainty of death, and so on. The office in choir, the conventual Mass, the conferences create the atmosphere of the retreat and I suppose the atmosphere is the retreat itself for no retreat Master can tell us anything new. I suppose that I could be a retreat Master without causing any damage.

TRAPPIST MONASTERY,
Wednesday, November 10, 1937 — 8:00 p.m.

Yesterday I offered up a Holy Hour twice for dad; today, twice for mother, tomorrow it will be twice for Sis. I made my confession today. I never expect to say Mass carelessly again nor ever again to entertain indecent thoughts though my confessor warned me that the devil seems to be working harder than ever.

Five times a day the retreat Master addresses us, most of the time for forty-five minutes. Though it has just struck 8 o'clock, I am physically exhausted and ready for a long sleep. The day is divided up by the various exercises so effectively that our minds are constantly occupied, especially if we work in a couple hours of adoration.

TRAPPIST MONASTERY,
Thursday, November 11, 1937 — 4:15 p.m.

The retreat Master is quite young. This retreat may be the first retreat that he ever gave to priests. His English is faulty until attention does not seem so keen. His thoughts seemed at first mediocre; today they were much deeper or I was not so critical. Could I have given this retreat? I could muster thoughts together for ten minutes at a time, but I certainly could not keep going for forty-five minutes as our retreat Master does, all on the Garden of Olives or the Scourging at the Pillar,

This morning, first conference was on obedience to our Bishop. Bishops may make mistakes, we never make a mistake in obeying him. The second conference was on the priesthood. Never do anything, say anything, go anywhere that is unbecoming of a priest, The third conference was on the Breviary. Saying the Breviary is never a waste of time. "Why this waste" was first asked by Judas when some precious thing was spent on our Lord.

LYNCH, KY., December 1, 1937

One year's cost record of operating automobile:

>Itemized cost — Ist year of a Dodge Coupe
>Two years cost of operating a Dodge Coupe.
>-Lynch, Ky., December 1, 1938
>Four years cost of operating a Dodge Coupe.
>-January 1, 1941
>67,000 in 49 months
>Including interest on investment, actual depreciation.
>Garage, insurance, cost of accidents, etc
>($810 less $375)
>$2,355 or
>$1.50 a day or
>3 1/2, a mile at 45 miles a day
>1941 — 4 passenger Coupe Plymouth with heater and Prestone
>Cost — $940 on January 1, 1941

The ratio of the cost of the car to its maintenance over the 49 month period was 1 to 4, *a brief diary of a Kentucky mountain missioner*

GETHSEMANI KY., November 9, 1938 -10:45 p.m.

My third retreat in this monastery, though it is almost half over already. We have the same retreat Master as last year, though his ideas are all fresh. One has no difficulty in listening to him for forty-five minutes five times a day.

The time is flying by. Never before have I made a retreat that did not drag. I find that I am not in the hurry I used to be. I don't drive so fast any more. I say Mass a little slower. In this my temperament is changing. I broke a spring on my car Monday; it delayed me three hours. Though I

THE KENTUCKY MOUNTAIN MISSION AREA

Ten years ago, (1988) the Diocese of Lexington was formed to include the many counties formerly served by the Covington Diocese. (Shaded area) To appreciate the distances Father Hanses often travelled, locate the cities and towns in their proper counties: Covington, the seat of the diocese in Kenton County; Ashland, a mission center in Boyd County; Corbin in Whitley County; Lexington, now a diocese in Fayette County; Himlerville, also called "Beauty" because the Hungarian population terraced the hills with flower beds, located in Martin County; Lynch in Harlan County where Fr. Hanses worked for more than 20 years; and Van Lear, where St. Casimir Mission Center was established. Father Hanses seems always to have been searching for the most economical automobile. How many thousands of miles he must have driven through the mountains of Eastern Kentucky.

knew I would be late for the retreat, I never drove over 60 miles an hour and I touched sixty only once to pass another car.

And so I find that there is nothing to do here at Gethsemani but to give myself to the order of the day.

3:00 p,m.

I made the Way of the Cross after dinner. I felt how rich I was in everything worthwhile. Who in this wide world has more than I have right now. To be sure, I have often played around with tinsel. In my heart I have broken every one of God's commandments, but by the grace of God, I am not conscious of having given scandal, especially to members of the other sex. But because of my many sins (interior sins against the virtue of purity) I resolve again, as a mortification, to stop smoking and every time I hunger for a smoke, I hope to be reminded of the sins I wish to atone for.

I used to pride myself on what I called my census work. The retreat Master today stressed the good of annual visitation among the pastor's flock. I resolve to take up this work again in earnest as soon as I return to Harlan County, to visit especially the lowliest in the parish on whatever pretext presents itself.

November 10, 1938 — 5:00 p,m.

The retreat is almost over. I resolved to say my daily rosary, if at all convenient, before the Blessed Sacrament in order to gain the Indulgences granted on that condition and to insure that it is said with proper devotion.

LYNCH, KY., Tuesday, July 30, 1940 — 9:00 p.m.

Mary Agnes, now almost 16, and her three brothers returned to Franklin today after a ten day visit with their daddy and step-mother who came only yesterday.

I wish to enter some prophecies on this occasion. I wish to look into the future, to present what is in store for Luella, the children's step-mother.

You get from the world what you give the world. If you want a friend, be a friend. Or, in still simpler words, two plus two make four.

Luella, so far as I can see, has made no effort to win Mary Agnes, has not even tried to analyze her, to understand her. Mary Agnes is cold, indifferent, not demonstrative. She shed scarce a tear when her mother died. She makes a fuss over no one. When Luella took seriously sick shortly after having become a step-mother, Mary Agnes ignored her; she was to Mary Agnes a stranger in the house. Luella has resented this ever since. Instead of trying to become a mother to Mary Agnes, she was determined from the beginning to have Mary Agnes swing the censor before her without first doing anything for Mary Agnes to suggest to Mary Agnes that she, Luella, was deserving of her love and respect,

This so far, seems narrow but I had a good opportunity to study Luella during the ten waking hours that we were in conversation. Luella called my attention to the fact that when Mary Agnes came into the house immediately after her and Joe's arrival, she failed to greet her, Luella. I, on the other hand, noticed that Luella failed to greet Mary Agnes. Who should have made the first move? Mary Agnes is shy; Luella mean, as I expect to show. The score in this encounter goes against Luella in view of the background of her recent vacation (New York and Washington alone) on which occasion she wrote to every member of the family except Mary Agnes.

I asked her and Joe to leave Mary Agnes with me, to make her home with me. Luella said that the matter was entirely up to the girl's father, knowing what answer Joe was going to give. When this suggestion was vetoed, I next proposed that Mary Agnes remain with me for the balance of the summer that I might have an opportunity to coach her in her Latin and Algebra, having almost failed in these subjects, Luella left down her guard. She did not say: It is up to Daddy. With a shake of the head, she said no; I'm not going to be tied down for a whole month, I need her. Mary Agnes gets less consideration from her than if she were a servant girl, Luella never intended to be a mother to Mary Agnes; she planned that Mary Agnes be a convenient tool. Luella made no attempt to prepare supper, wash the dishes or put the little ones to bed, though she did fry some potatoes,

She had not a kind word for Mary Agnes. She referred to the letter that Mary Agnes wrote to her daddy a few days ago. She spoke of it derogatively several times; how a girl could write that way to her daddy, that she can't write a better letter than that, that she can't use more correct grammar and punctuation. But I happen to know that that letter was written to Mr. & Mrs. Joseph Fedders and began with the words: Dear Daddy and Mother — not only because I saw the letter and know also that I dictated it and know also that the letter was begun over four times including the original. Luella is determined to make Mary Agnes miserable. She will not succeed. She is only sowing trouble for herself. Luella is a stranger to Mary Agnes and always will be. Mary Agnes has an excellent chance of taking care of herself in life. Luella will spend her time in sourly pointing out Mary Agnes' cruelty to her but she will refuse to recognize that Mary Agnes' bitterness is only the effect of causes established by Luella.

I was quite blue when the family first left, but I feel better now. It is much better for Mary Agnes to have a servant girl career in her life than to be pampered always and continually by folks like me. Mary Agnes came through all right.

But Joe is destined to be nagged in his old age; his present married life is destined to be a very dull one, an unhappy one. Still it has this bright side — he appreciates now like he never did before what a real Christian wife he had in Sis. Fuss they did and quarrel, and they thought at times that they were miserable, but now Joe sees that they never once disagreed in vital matters, that they were a real team, that they worked and suffered and lived and died for a common purpose — the children that God gave them. Imagine Sis complaining about (not to say anything about refusing) being tied down by her obligations to her family!

GETHSEMANI, Tuesday, August 26, 1941 — 10:40 a.m.

I arrived yesterday evening with Father Ryan, for my fourth retreat at Gethsemani. I read over the account of previous retreats as contained in this diary and note that the first words in the book are "Father Spain," who died since our last retreat or just before. My last retreat was at Mt. Airy with Uncle, where I have been three times for private retreats.

I note also in my first account in this book how the priests around me appeared smug, well fed, prosperous. I don't see the same things in the present group, about fifteen of us who, for some reason or other, could not attend the main diocesan retreat held in St. Gregory's in June. These fifteen are fellows that you don't hear much about, that are not famous for doing big things, at least who do not say so themselves. There are two Monsignors, Leich and Hillenmeyer, and you can see that they are determined to set a good example. Are they not Monsignors specially honored by Bishop and Pope? No, no. Fathers Hillenmeyer and Leich would act just exactly like they are acting if they were simple priests. I don't know of any four Monsignors — and we now have more — who have been puffed up by their new dignity and perhaps that is why they have been selected from among us for such honor. Then there are with us simple folks like Fathers Poole, Nienaber, Wimmers, Fischer, Donovan, Whalen — these are not fifteen — the skinniest bunch of priests I have seen at prayer with me, biggest in the bunch, weighing over 210.

We have again the same retreat Master. It is the third time I have sat at his feet and I do not recall that he has ever repeated himself. His conferences are plenty long and interesting, However, he gives us enough matter at each conference to do for the whole retreat. At each talk I try to get a hold on the central thought or at least on a main thought and then make not much effort to hold on any more, His opening shot was "How much of each day do I give to God. Look over the big cities, the avenues, cross streets, alleys, hotels, apartment houses, business offices, houses of amusement — how much time or thought are the people concerned giving to God, But priests? Certainly they are making up for a cold and indifferent people. Are they? How much of my time do I give to God?"

His meditation this morning hinged on this thought, Live for the next world, not for this one, Vacations, trips, amusement, smoking, drinking can easily take us out of the next work and put us in this one,

2:00 p.m.

Today's examen centered on Judas, In his boyhood, he was a likable lad. Our Lord saw something in him, entrusted him with His funds and the management of His affairs. Judas was a good business man, reliable, honest, until he quit examining his conscience!! In our daily examination, concentrate especially on de sexto and focus attention always on two things — resist beginnings — avoid occasions.

Wednesday — 4:30 p.m.

I have just been to confession. Every time (except one) I have been to Gethsemani I have gone to confession to Father Poole. The Trappists frightened me. They hear about three confessions an hour and they work so hard on their penitents, the confessionals are strewn all over the church and you see the confessors working with both hands. And then I found out that it takes twenty minutes for Father Poole to settle with me and he can work with everything that God gave him.

I told Father Poole that I would have been better off if I had died five years ago, still better off if I had died ten years ago and still better off had I died fifteen years ago. I said that I hoped I was not going down hill; that the next five, ten, fifteen years would find me pulling a strong stroke back up the stream. I was told, among other things, that I had forgotten that my main office was to say Mass.

9:00 p.m.

In tonight's conference, we were told that you never hear of a Jesuit knocking another Jesuit, or a Franciscan another Franciscan, Why should not secular priests have *Esprit-de-corps* also towards one another and towards their Bishop

Thursday — 10:30 a.m.

In a half hour, we gather for a Holy Hour, then dinner, then dismissal. Father Ryan will return with Father Fischer to London where the three of us will meet at London Hall for supper. Then Father Ryan will proceed to Lynch with me where he left his car and Father Fischer will cut across country to Hazard.

One of the Trappist took us through the Monastery. I had noticed in the main corridor that all the pictures on the walls were Madonnas. In another section of the Monastery, the cloister or rather the section reserved for the monks that all the pictures were of ancient cathedrals and monasteries. Only then did I get the idea of bordering the walls of the classrooms of the Cumberland School with pictures of the world's church monument. I would like also to get in a set of the more gripping Madonnas. We will see. I will study the matter closely, nothing haphazard.

I leave now spiritually refreshed, bodily rested and eager to get back to work. I have always maintained that vacations were a matter of the mind, that one could take a vacation anywhere at any time when one made up his mind to do so. Like the Trappist, the only vacations I want from now on will be in monasteries.

MT. AIRY, Wednesday, May 20, 1942 — 8:00 a.m.

Uncle and I arrived here Monday before dinner for a retreat. It is my fifth at Mt. Airy. Uncle said he made his first retreat here in 1911. I made my first one here in 1920.

I am making a vacation out of this visit rather than a retreat. I felt the need of a change for the past few months more than ever before, When, oh when, I have been asking myself, will I wake up on a Sunday morning with an unclouded mind? I can't feel that way now. Usually a retreat is a period of strain. I am completely relaxed this time. May the Lord forgive me! There was a time when retreat meant an hour's adoration for Dad, another for Mother, another for Sis and then all over again. This time I made an hour during High Mass yesterday, I'll make another one after my confession at 9:00. this morning.

We, Uncle and I, have spent much of the time together. We enjoyed, for example, a two hour walk around the grounds after supper last night. He is now 72 and says he thinks of death every day. He looks as if he has twenty years of work in him yet. Almost constantly he is telling me what a comfort I am to him, how good God has been to him and so on. If my disposition, personality is such as to give joy to others by my presence, I must keep myself conscious of the peculiar gifts God has given me and use them as He would have me do. But one hand washes the other; two and two make four; as we sow, so shall we reap. I am giving back to Uncle only what he has given to me. It took us years of separation to get the right perspective. When I was near him, I saw in him many weaknesses; I thought him tight, even cruel. Now I recognize more than ever before that though scores have been good to me, it's no use trying to list them, Uncle stepped in and reestablished the home for mother and took my father's place in my regard. And today, with mother gone and Sis gone and no one left in Uncle's immediate family who now needs my help, he entrusts me with everything that he has left for me to use as he would use it.

Since my last retreat, I have rebelled against authority, I have been telling myself that the fourth commandment works two ways, that I don't owe respect where respect is not given. I have expected the Bishop to be loyal to me before I am loyal to him. I must try to learn the lesson of one hand working the other; I get what I ask for; if I want to be treated like a pastor who can be trusted, I must act like one. For the good of religion, I must study my man and handle him so that he will hand it back to me as I want. This I want to make the principal fruit of my retreat,

ST. MARY'S ROLAND PARK, BALTIMORE,
Monday, August 23, 1943 — 10:00 p.m.

I arrived at the Seminary early this morning with Father Kraus of Norton, Va. for a retreat. Our diocesan priests are to make their retreat privately this year. I chose to make mine with the Wheeling priests.

We had breakfast in the Pennsylvania depot and then walked down Charles Street, past the Cardinal's residence, then to the Cathedral. Then over to Paca Street where we found alligators, snakes, mice, etc. in the former philosopher's chapel, now a science room, the fifth floor closed and the whole building quite run down in anticipation of moving the rest of the Seminary to Roland Park. At dinner I saw Fr. Haney and Fr. Hunalt, Fr. Reilly and Fr. Lavatois are still on the job. After dinner, I tried to make reservations for our return by plane Friday but all seats were sold out. We bought railroad tickets. After that we took a taxi to St. Charles, inspected the whole of it without encountering a single priest. Most of the dead in the cemetery, among them my former confessors, Fathers Duffy, Boyer, Harig, were associated with my student life.

After supper I had a nice walk with Fr. Quinn. I saw Fr. Halsley in the chapel.

A Redemptorist is conducting the retreat. His opening gun was that grace was the living in the friendship of God; this is a time of grace; anticipate the joy, the fact that we are to spend a week with our best friend.

Wednesday, August 25, 1943 — 10:25 p.m.

I just finished the Life of Father Damien. I won't feel like sleeping for a while. Reading about Father Damien has kept me from recording my retreat impressions. For the sake of the record, I put down this thought the retreat Master has emphasized several times — Love of God means loyalty to Him, the Latin we have would be better translated by Loyalty.

Twenty-five years ago, I was just becoming used to being a sub-deacon and getting ready to begin my last year in the seminary. I don't know of a better way of celebrating a silver jubilee than the manner in which I am now celebrating it, the twenty-fifth anniversary of my having been accepted by the Church, If there is to be any censor swinging before me, it will be none of my planning. The keynote of this occasion is: *"Quid retribuam Domino pro omnibus quae retribuit mihi?"* All my life I have had better breaks than I deserved.

Here I write, a seminarian again in spirit. Twenty-five years ago I said my breviary during Father Reilly's scripture classes, paying no attention to Fr. Reilly. The thought of this plagues me now as I see Fr. Reilly from time to time going down the corridor. On my last night at the Seminary, at the end of the last recreation period, Fr. Brianceau said: "By the way, Mr. Hanses, I can't find your liturgy examination paper anywhere; what happened to it?" The bell struck for silence. I had skipped the examination due to my early departure for ordination. I wonder if Fr. Brianceau, as he passed me now, is still waiting for an answer. In Canon Law examination, Fr. Lavatois gave me a 4; as he sees me now, does he remember me as a study of great promise? Father Bruno, long since dead, said of me a generation ago: he takes too many liberties on the grounds of ill health. All my life I have had better breaks than I deserve.

The new Seminary at Roland Park does not arouse any feelings of jealousy. My room is screened, my desk is a desk, not a table; the room is furnished with a bookcase, closet and running water; the floor is of cork. The grounds are beautiful, the playing courts are modern, the meals are sumptuous. But the new Seminary does not have Father Dyer, who would pause after giving us a tongue lashing and then remark: "After all, I guess it's my fault; I have not been praying for you as I should".

So many people lean on me for support today, parishioners, nuns, and even brother priests of the mountains. Whence comes that which strengthens me? I have broken every one of God's commandments, if not in deed then in my heart. I have committed every sin except one, by the grace of God; I am not conscious of ever having given scandal. Fr, Byer's best remembered admonition is: Never touch a woman! Thanks to you, Father Dyer, for your earnest admonition and your prayers. I have never playfully, familiarly touched a woman!

I record here a portion of Stephenson's defence of Damien against the charge by Rev. Dr. Hyde to the effect that Damien had not been a "pure man in his relations with women."

"I will suppose your story to be true. I will suppose — and God forgive me for supposing it — that Damien faltered and stumbled in his narrow path of duty; I will suppose that in the horror of his desolation, perhaps in the fever of incipient disease, he who was doing so much more than he had sworn, failed in the letter of his priestly oaths — he who was so much a better man than either you or me, who did what we have never dreamed of daring — he too tasted of our common frailty." O Lago, the pity of it! The least tender should be moved to tears, the most incredulous to prayer. And all that you could do was to pen your letter to the Rev. H. B. Gage! (Ave Maria Press — publication.)

LYNCH, KY., Monday, April 10, 1944 — 11:15 p.m,

For the sake of the record, I make this entry while the memory of the affair is fresh in my memory. A few weeks ago, a government commissioner entered Saulino's establishment in Cumberland to make an investigation regarding the employment and pay of women workers. He found a woman employee, Mrs. Perry, colored. After interrogating her, he reported that Saulino employed a female whom he worked from 6:00 to 6:00, who was so busy that she took no time out for lunch but ate a sandwich when she had a chance, that according to him, Saulino had no record of hours worked, that Mrs. Perry did not know how much she was making because her wages were handed to her husband on pay day. The commissioner further reported, a copy of which Judge Fiester showed me, that he never heard of such a case in his life. Subsequently, three charges were filed against Saulino and April 10th set for a hearing.

Mrs. Perry, Saulino and I appeared at City Hall at the appointed time. The commissioner throughout the hearing was more interested in convincing himself and us that Saulino had violated O.P.A. regulations rather than in getting the facts. The commissioner first read what he said were the facts as given to him by Mrs, Perry. He then asked her: "Are these statements true or not? Yes or no." Mrs. Perry answered: "I told you that I get up at 6:00 o'clock and about 7:30 I go over to the shop. No one ever told me what time to go to work or what time to quit. The work I was paid for takes about three or four hours to do and when I am through, I go into the back and help my husband at his work — he is old and feeble." To which the commissioner answered: "After you spilled the beans, you now want to cover up. No, I'll take that back — I should not say you spilled the beans. Whether you get paid by the day or on commission makes no difference; you are not allowed to work more than nine hours a day or sixty hours a week and your employer violated the regulations because he did not keep your time and he violated regulations when he handed your pay to your husband even if most of the time he handed your husband's pay to you." After a lot more to-do-about-nothing, he said he was willing to recommend the minimum fine if Saulino chose not to fight the case and Saulino paid $25.00 and $8.50 cost because he failed to keep a daily record of Mrs. Perry's beginning and ending work though Mrs. Perry was not permitted to say that she never worked longer hours than the regulations permitted, and because occasionally Saulino handed her pay to her husband.

Walter McCurry listened to the proceedings. Later he told me his story. O.P.A. men stopped in at the Cliff House a few days ago and paid $5.00 for a pint of whiskey. Whereupon the proprietor was arrested. He was told, however, if he reported where he got his whiskey — he squealed on McCurry. Then McCurry was told that he faced the possibility of a $1,000 fine for selling liquor wholesale without a license because he had sold a case to the Cliff House. McCurry asked for the number of the case he was charged with having sold to the Cliff House. It was given to him. The record showed that McCurry bought the liquor in November 1943 and was a part of the stock that was stolen from him in December 1943. (It is common knowledge that McCurry high-jacked himself after having sold $4,000 worth of whiskey to boot-leggers who were to take it out of his place in small lots.) Thereupon, McCurry told the O.P.A. if the charges were not dropped, he would charge the Cliff House with selling stolen whiskey. The charges were dropped.

MELBOURNE, KY., Wednesday, June 12, 1946 — 3:45 p.m.

Am making my retreat with the junior half of the clergy, Only two of the fifty priests here this week are senior to me, Fathers Streck and Nurre. I am so far advanced in the priesthood that work left undone by me will be brought to a finish by men already now experienced in the priesthood. I am no longer just getting started, Much of the work assigned to me has already been finished. My youth is behind me, God has been good to me. May I not be a disappointment to Him in the more mellow days of my seniority.

I came Monday afternoon with Fathers Ryan, Middendorf, Mueller. My last retreat was at Mt. Airy last fall with uncle, during a mission at St. John's. The year before that I joined the priests of the Wheeling diocese in Baltimore. It has been almost five years since I made a retreat with the Covington priests.

Bishop Mulloy opened up the retreat Monday night by trying to be tough. He wanted to show how fearless he was. Everybody comes before me. I shrivel them all up. In spite of three and a half hours recreation every day, two after dinner, the rest after supper, there is as much levity as ever I have seen at a retreat, except in the refectory under the Bishop's eye. There has been a DON'T-GIVE-A-DAMN Atmosphere since the Bishop's opening talk, though the talk may not be the occasion of the atmosphere. Perhaps it's only subjective. Perhaps it's only me. I have, however, not given any bad example.

The retreat Master is dull. But, after all, why should a retreat Master be other than dull? What is there new that he can tell us? He is there simply to think out loud for us. His opening theme was; a retreat was a time for us to get better acquainted with Our Lord. In his morning conference yesterday, he exhorted us to have more of Mary and less of Martha in us. Less of worrying about the work assigned to us and more of tending to our own business. In the afternoon yesterday, he told us that no man ever habitually kept on the safe side of the line between mortal and venial sin without eventually crossing the line.

I'm sitting on the ground in the woods as I write these lines. The mosquitoes are eating me — the first time mosquitoes have bothered me in many years. Still I kid myself that the life in the wide open spaces is the life for me.

I can't recall much of what the retreat Master had to say so far today. We should look at the ordo before beginning Mass; we should tuck a handkerchief up our sleeve before going to the altar; and we should not deliberately sleep over on a Sunday morning or send mothers with crying babies out of church.

In another talk, he said that all authority came from God. And I thought of the assistant who took his orders from the housekeeper while the pastor took a trip to Germany. Well you should not be reading this.

MELBOURNE, Thursday, June 13, 1946 — 10:00 a.m

We have had one hot day during this retreat. Last night we had a refreshing rain. We have no desks in our rooms. I stand in the cemetery using a tombstone for my writing table.

I have had an ugly mood until this morning, I have made my Holy hour and have been to confession and am ready for another year.

Again, I'm quitting smoking, It's the easiest thing to do, I have been doing it so often.

The neon sign reads, "We may doze but never close!" From 1946 Captain Morton Chapman and his wife Virginia kept that motto, feeding the poor Father Hanses would send them a block from the church, each one with his voucher Father Henry distributed wholesale. The Captain, now 86 is looking for a buyer.

I'm renewing my resolution to make a weekly Holy hour of adoration and it's going to be on Monday after dinner or on the first day after that that is opportune.

The principal fruit of this retreat is the resolution to mind my own business. I'm going to quit squawking and belly-aching, I'm going to mind my own business and keep my mouth shut — like Father Deye, Middendorf and Streck.

COVINGTON, July 1, 1946 — 10:00p.m.

The only fear I had in accepting my appointment to St. John's last August was that as uncle grew older, he might weaken mentally in the direction of believing that I was planning to undermine him.

Little things appear like mountains sometimes and also sometimes they may point a direction. The last thing I wish to do is to cause uncle pain. In sheer defense of what may seem as cruelty on my part, I will record some of the things that to me seem to be pointers.

On Saturday (June 29) at a wedding dinner, the groom asked me, who was sitting closer to him than uncle, whether he should get proof of his marriage before setting out on his honeymoon. I said that I would see to it in time. Later, when I asked uncle for the certificate, I was told that the groom should have asked the pastor for it, I had to call in the groom and explain to him that he would have to call on the pastor for the certificate.

At 9:00 the same evening, the phone rang; uncle, as always, answered. A lady asked for me and explained to me that she was new in the parish and asked when she could have her baby baptized. I gave her the time and then explained to uncle what happened. Very much irritated, he snapped at me that I should have referred her to the pastor.

The day Mrs. O'Dom called me up to find out when she could see me, I made an appointment for the evening and in the evening left word with Elizabeth that if Mrs. O'Dom called, she could find me in the hall. When she arrived, uncle met her at the door, insulted her with some remark about preferring to deal with a young priest and ended by stating that Father Hanses was not here. Just then, Elizabeth delivered my message and Mrs. O'Dom came to the hall all upset because she couldn't understand what she had done to upset Father Goebel.

July 9, 1946 — 9:00 a.m.

On the train from Harlan last night, James McCarthy said to me: "I tried to get you on the phone about a week ago and I'll never call that number again. Three times I asked for you and three times I was told — this is Father Goebel speaking. He wanted to know who I was and what I wanted and wouldn't tell me when I could talk to you. I'll never call that number again."

A few minutes ago, at breakfast, the phone rang. I took the call. Sister Elizabeth Marie's sister said: "I've been trying to get you for a week, After an extended conversation, I sat down to breakfast again and said nothing about the call. After a minute or so, uncle curtly inquired: "Was that a woman who called — a woman of the parish?"

July 10 — 1:00 p.m.

Sister Marcella called today. Uncle took the call and handed me the phone. When he learned who it was, he said: "Now why did she have to change her voice?"

August 22

I am in favor of simplification in the matter of parish societies — one for the men, one for the women, one for the boys, one for the girls. In the case of the women's societies, nothing has been changed but the names, the one is now the Confraternity of Christian Doctrine, the other the Sodality of the Blessed Virgin. Secondly, uncle has consented to my suggestion that society dues be not used for revenue, that each society does what it pleases with its resources. The Sodality is paying for the publication of the parish bulletin. Along comes a crank who has belonged to the Young Ladies Sodality for a half-century; she objects to the Sodality making use of her dollar in any other way than it has been done in years past — it is to be given to the Church. She pulls the right stops and plays the right swells and now we have a Confraternity of the Blessed Sacrament for those unmarried ladies who do not wish to belong to the Sodality, though uncle is urging individual Sodality girls to join both the Confraternity of the Blessed Sacrament, as well as the Sodality.

The Sodality and the basketball team are planning a dance to raise funds for sending delegates to a Catholic Action School and for basketball suits. They had a meeting last night and though such things are in my province, uncle, without saying anything to me, tells the dance planners that they must break up the dance at 11:45, deliberately trying to throw cold water on their enthusiasm,

January 23, 1947

Bob Lange, basketball coach, called for me yesterday. Uncle told him to hold the phone. After fifteen minutes, Bob hung up.

MELBOURNE, KY., June 10, 1947 — 8:45 a.m.

Retreat. Fifty priests attending, Father McDonald, Sulpician, conducting. Bishop participating — as well as in last week's retreat.

Father McDonald is very good, though very dry. In his opening talk he stressed the importance of not permitting ourselves to become familiar with sacred things. Also, to accept people as we find them, not as we think they ought to be.

The point I liked best about this morning's meditation is that Christ used the way of death, not of power to accomplish his purpose.

NEWPORT CATHOLIC HIGH RETREAT, April 12-14, 1947

A. Duties towards God — B. Duties towards neighbor — C. Duties towards self.

A. 1. Be eager to get close to God. You can lead a horse to water but you can't make him drink. Give yourself generously — negatively by not disturbing others; positively by being recollectful; your exterior reflecting your interior. Where does a retreat fit in a High School year? Confessions after last confessions. Written questions answered.

A, 2, Existence of God
"Don't believe what you preach,"
Uncaused cause. From effect to cause.
What tremendous things man has accomplished.
Elevator signals; 40 times a second combustion.
But all the scientists in the world — a grain of wheat.
Daily prayers — morning and night.

A. 3. Duties as a group.
Mass — the center of the day.   Benediction;
Don't sandwich it in.   Novenas;
Go up front.   Rosary.
Pray the Mass.

B. 1. Duties as a family
Rosary or wash dishes.
Know its members — Sis, Brothers, Grandma,
Indulgences — Way of the Cross.

B. 2. Duties toward others
We are our brothers' keeper,
Parents — kin — and neighbors.
Love is giving, not getting.
Look to duties more than right.
Human nature best in adversity.
We can't stand prosperity.

B. 3. Girl friends
1. Mixed marriage.

2. Like daughter, like wife.
  3. Stay on God's side.
C. 1. Duties toward self
  Know self.
  Respect self.
  Knowledge — Everything you have was given you;
  Best catches from another shoulders;
  Therefore, humility,
  Respect — Vessel of honor;
  Don't be a pig.

C, 2. Are Catholic boys better than non-Catholics?
  If not, confession and Communion don't mean anything.
  Confession — don't make a mockery;
  Communicn — God and I can do anything.

C. 3. Things to be thankful for,

MELBOURNE, Thursday, June 8, 1948 — 8:30 a.m.

I notice that I did not keep any retreat notes last year. I remember the retreat Master, Father McDonald, S.S., a junior school-mate of Seminary days. He was pretty good- Take people as you find them was his theme. Simple enough. Don't try to make them over into what you would like to have them be.

This year's retreat Master is a Canadian Jesuit. One must make an effort to understand him. His opening shot was that we are not in heaven yet, that this retreat was a help to assure heaven. Dying a happy death is a matter of living right. Most people die unexpectedly, unprepared; those who die in a coma die as unexpectedly as those who die suddenly.

His theme this morning was that everybody who takes life seriously means business at retreat time. The Pope makes retreats — Cardinals — monks — nuns.

There comes to my mind Bishop Howard addressing us at a retreat opening. He said that if we wanted individually to do a favor for the diocese, we could do nothing better than make a good retreat.

In his morning conference, the retreat Master emphasized that we are God's completely, nothing of ourselves is ours (except sin), everything comes from Him, is His. Why then must I have such a hard time to adjust myself. I am a frustrated old maid, I am His, Uncle is His. Bishop Mulloy is His. St. John's — Harlan, I must tell myself this over and over and then must start all over again. If I don't adjust myself, is my mind out of gear?

4:15 p.m.

St. Ignatius: TANTUM, QUANTUM; all material things were created for our benefit, positively or negatively. Insofar as they help us attain our end, union with God, they are for us to use. Insofar as they hinder us to attain our end, they are to be avoided. Therefore, we are not to long for health rather than sickness, wealth rather than poverty, a long life rather than an early death, preferment rather than obscurity, one post rather than another.

Wednesday — 11:00 a,m.

The retreat Master has been trying hard to scare us with his description of hell. For an hour last night, he had fallen angels, four abreast from here to New York, walking, falling into the pit. Today, again, it was smoke and slime and monstrous things,

Such ideas never make any impression on me. We can't get any notion of the pains of hell, of the enormity of sin any more than we can understand the bliss of the Blessed. Hell to me simply means failure, everything that I do not want. If I do want to get some idea of its misery, nothing impresses me like the thought of mental torture: God was unfair; He did not give me a chance; He played favorites; He created me simply to torture!!!!!

I made my annual confession this morning, Oscar Poole, the closest thing to a Cure of Ars I have ever known, shrived me,

Thursday — 6:40 a.m.

Yesterday afternoon, the R. M. compared the universe to God; the earth to the universe; myself to the earth.

I was told that I was a microbe, an insignificant in that the world was not depending on me.

In the afternoon, the talk was on the Passion, what Our Lord did for me. The Circumcision would have been enough; an hour in the carpenter shop. But no, according to Newman, nothing worthwhile is accomplished without suffering. Our Lord suffered.

By way of reparation to the Sacred Heart and Father Brinker's request, I made a Holy Hour during the middle of last night and the night before. I offered these periods in reparation for my carelessness at Mass, for too much attention paid to the stipend. At each station, I prayed that that station be accepted by way of reparation for a specific poor Soul. Each decade of the rosary was offered up by way of reparation for a living person or a group of persons.

I don't know who else made hours except those who were before and after me. As I was preparing to serve Alfred's Mass this morning, he asked:

Were you up during the night? I am going to ask him to try Nocturnal Adoration.

LAY RETREAT GIVEN AT VILLA MADONNA, July 15-18, 1948

Thursday night.
We are here to commune with God.

Ist. Leave the world outside; the best thing that you can do for your family is to make a good retreat.

2nd. Relax. Physically, mentally. When the right idea strikes, hold on to it. Diary.

3rd. Cooperate. Silence. No hen parties.

Outline — Faith, Hope, Charity.

Theme — We are children of God and heirs of heaven.

Friday morning.

Faith — definition.

Faith in the natural order.

Faith in the supernatural order takes up where science and philosophy leave off,

Conclusion — To whom shall we go, if not,...

Friday afternoon.

God is our authority. The Church is our teacher.

Infallibility, a necessity — our comfort,

Sin of indifference.

Friday night,

Symbols of our faith. The sign of the cross. Faith and Benediction.

Saturday morning.

Hope — definition — desire God as our highest good, firm confidence, eternal happiness. because of God's goodness and power.

Despair — Judas, Extreme Unction.

Presumption.

Dante "Abandon hope all ye who enter here."

Dies Irae: Mihi quoque spem dedisti.

Saturday night.

Rosary.

Sunday

Charity — love God for His own sake and man for God's sake.

St. Therese and the mouth of hell.

Fellow man — Golden Rule.
2nd degree: Reparation Nocturnal Adoration.

Afternoon

Keep a balance between the needs of the body and the needs of the soul.
Questions
Can you give me some pointers on the nature of a religious vocation?
Sister Grace — Father Dyer,
What is a person to do about the deluge of alm's requests through mail?
We take with us only what we give away.

What is the best approach to non-Catholic loved ones when you want to share your faith?

Never argue.

Does one receive as much protection from a four-way medal bracelet as from a medal worn about the neck?

Gas saving gadget.

Please tell me how to recognize the difference between mortal and venial sin, Is it a mortal sin to be ashamed to pray at your meals in public?

My husband earns $40 dollars a week; we have three children. Do we offend God if we practice birth control? to give our children a fair chance?

Is it a sin to read others' mail through curiosity?

Why do people strike their breasts?

Tell us about indulgences.

If sponsors can make a profession of faith for infants, why can't a mother procure baptism of desire for her dying child?

MARRIED LADIES RETREAT, WEST COVINGTON, March 6, 1949

1. Where there are two or three gathered together in my name, there I am in the midst of them. Commune with God. What is to be said is not important, Silence could serve the same purpose. However, I'll keep rambling along. One thought will appeal to one, another to another,..,Who is God? Who am I? How sublime our faith! How fortunate we are in having an infallible teacher! It's almost too good to be true. God, out of sheer goodness, gave me existence.

2. What shall it profit a man if he gain the whole world. Half animal and half spirit. Must take care of both but must keep the proper perspective. Bill Meiners — the thing that worried him was only money. If his wife had run off with another man, if his son had become a scoundrel, then he would have something to worry about. If Junior breaks an arm, if brother burns a hole in the carpet, try an act of contrition. If all's right with God, nothing else matters.

3. Prayer. Thy Will, not mine. Pray for courage to see that it is in God's hands that guides everything that happens. Family prayers — the Rosary, Invite the departed into your circle.

MELBOURNE ANNUAL RETREAT,
Thursday, June 15, 1950 — 10:00 a.m.

Father Bondy, O.S.B. of Toronto, retreat Master. Very good. Have had no pep whatever. Third day of the retreat and have not yet made the Way of the Cross.

One cannot be a spiritually minded priest if he is a regular reader of light literature. Meditate daily. Don't worry about method. A good teacher, regardless of pedagogy, is one who communicates himself to his pupils. The matter of meditating is the fruit of one's own meditating. Pick out a subject the night before. Spiritual reading from fifteen to thirty minutes a day. Work hard at it; don't look for anything light or sentimental. TRY THE SUMMA in English.

MELBOURNE ANNUAL RETREAT,
Thursday, June 5, 1951 — 3:00 p.m.

Retreat Master, Father John McCarthy, head of the Chicago Diocesan Retreat House. Very good.

On the day of my ordination, I did not speculate whether the man next to me would get ahead of me. I wanted the future tough, as a challenge to my generosity. Let that man preach the retreat to you.

Spiritual reading. Try a life of Christ. Picture to yourself some event in Christ's life and then try to foresee some event in the day that might parallel that event, determine to act as Christ would in your place,

June 5 — 8:45 p.m.

Instead of commanding Christ with the words: "This is My Body," let's make a covenant with Him by way of making our body His: these are your hands, this is your mouth, lips, tongue, These are your feet, So many people see God in us; let it be really so: "I live, now not I, but Christ lives in Me."

MELBOURNE ANNUAL RETREAT, May 31, 1954

Arrived Sunday night, yesterday, exhausted. Have been waiting for this get-away-from-it-all since uncle's death in January; the new broom alterations, assistant, housekeeper, Lent, investiture reception, Alfred's breakdown, picnic and grade graduation (on May 29 and 30). Went to bed at 7:30, skipped the opening exercise, got a telephone call which I ignored, slept till 6:00 this morning; the best sleep I remember ever to have had since I left the mountains almost nine years ago. For the first time since then, do I care to keep a real diary retreat.

I asked Alfred this morning to brief me on what I missed in the opening talk. The retreat Master's theme was: be not a man of God but God's man.

This first talk this morning was on practicing death. You never do anything just right the first time whether it's a game or a sermon or a trip. But you die only once. We will never get a chance to improve on it. But we can practice it. Put ourselves on a death bed, tired, worried sick; then in the coffin; then in the grave and judgment.

His second talk: teaching does not do any good unless you prove what you say by your living. Two powers are given the priest; that of forgiving sins and that of saying Mass. We cannot say: I'll accept the powers but do not choose to live the life,

No one is hated and loved more than the priest, like no one was hated and loved more than Christ. Why is a priest loved? There are others in the community who are more cultured or more learned than he, The priest is loved because Christ is in him.

We must be Christ-centered,

His next two talks were dull: sin and hell. I guess I'm too smug. I'll have to concentrate on these matters. The talk on sin was divided into three chapters: the sin of the angels, the sin of our first parents and our personal sins.

Hell was a place of fire, darkness and companionship with reprobates, What kind of fire — no one knows. Every other week we learn something about fire. The world would like the words sin and hell omitted from the dictionary.

June 1, Tuesday

His first talk this morning was tops. Am I more interested in the morning or was the topic more interesting? And is it proper for the pupil to pass judgment on the work of his teacher unless he knows more than the teacher? Is it ever proper to "enjoy" a sermon? Is there not something to be learned out of even the mediocre sermon? The speaker said in a previous talk that since God's truths are eternal, they are eternally new and every time we contemplate a truth, it leaves something new,

This morning's talk was on God's mercy toward priests. He told the story of Peter and Thomas. After Peter sinned, he was forgiven; if he had to do penance for the rest of his life, he would have been eternally grateful; if he had been reinstated as an Apostle, he would have regarded himself unworthy. But he was reinstated as the head of the Church, Why? Because Our Lord did not look on the sin but what was in his heart. When Our Lord looks at a priest, he sees in him the eager altar boy that he was, the fervent seminarian, the ardent newly ordained.

I hope so. It was nice of the speaker to be so gracious. It is not for me to question him as it is not proper for my penitents to question my counsel. I have always leaned to the generous side and have sometimes wondered whether I should not have emphasized the *tutior pars*. After this morning's talk, I am confirmed in my generous outlook. However, though I may not go to hell because of past sins, there is no assurance that the next sin won't be my undoing. In the talk on Hell he said: Ask a condemned soul how he got to where he was and he will answer: I sinned and was forgiven and sinned again and I happened to be called after having sinned and before I was forgiven.

4:00 p.m.

The morning talk and the afternoon talk moved me like no other talk in recent memory.

A priest should go to confession every week or two and he should take a half hour to prepare himself for it. Sure, absolution works *ex opere operato* but there is an *ex opere operantis* that goes along Confession as a Sacrament. Mass is, of course, first in importance; in a priest's life, the Sacrament of Penance should come second. The preparation could be the morning's meditation. A priest making such use of this Sacrament will never omit his meditation, will be recollected at Mass, will be good to the weak and oppressed, will control his temper.

The afternoon talk was on mental prayer, a half hour's meditation, in a prayerful attitude before Mass. Distractions are in the mind but if the will is in control, distractions won't spoil the half hour given to God. Method is not prayer. Prayer is love. The sign of the cross, the prayers of the Mass, the New Testament, the following of Christ — any of these could form the basis of mental prayer, THREE THINGS: TIME, EFFORT, PERSEVERANCE.

To think that I used to be that way. I used to be on my knees from 5:30 to 6:00. I used to go to confession weekly to Father DeSmet, I got away from it when I went on the missions — I don't know why. I see no reason for not getting back in the groove again right now.

June 2

Our night's talk was on suffering and this morning's meditation on the Mass. I'll pass up those two to leave the emphasis on the weekly confession and daily half hour meditation before Mass. I asked Father Finn this morning to be my regular confessor and he generously planned to stop at St. John's rectory every Friday morning on his way to the Chancery. I am looking forward to a new pace which was old-stuff to me many years ago, Nothing succeeds like success — it's easy to be good when you're good.

MARYDALE ANNUAL RETREAT, April 27, 1955

Eighteen of us, including the Bishop, are making our retreat at Marydale to release somewhat the crowded conditions at Melbourne. We can't figure out the basis of selection — are we the elite or are we the bad apples that have to be removed from the regular group?

The retreat Master is a Franciscan. In his opening talk, he told us that we should not thank God that we are not like the rest of men. And right now, the morning after, I can't think of another thing he said. My memory is going back on me, physically I am deteriorating; time is short, what I want to do I had better be doing.

The first talk this morning was on faith. Agnoscite quod agitis. Faith shows the world from a different prospective like the microscope puts the drop of water or the telescope the sky above in entirely new light.

When an engineer is taking his train on a run, he is not interested in the scenery, in the character of his passengers. He watches the signals, keeps his destination in mind, keeps his schedule, watches his instruments............God is the only thing I want. I am not interested in creatures, in comfort, in the kind of work I am doing, in health or wealth but I am living only for God.

The retreat Master quotes copiously from scriptures and the encyclicals. I was surprised how he could make these authorities suit his purpose so fittingly. On the matter of frequent confessions, he quotes from Mystici Corporis Christi: By frequent confession, genuine self-knowledge is increased. Christian humility grows, bad habits are corrected, spiritual neglect and tepidity are countered, the conscience is purified, the will strengthened, a salutary self-control is attained and grace is increased in virtue of the Sacrament itself.

This quotation sent me to the encyclical itself and I find it more readable than I ever found an encyclical before.

His talk on poverty also impressed me. He quoted the capitulum of today's Lauds, *"confessor non pontiff. Beatus vir"*. That's all of the Latin I can give from memory. I have a feeling that this capitulum henceforth will always remind me of this retreat and particularly of what poverty should mean to a priest.

MILFORD ANNUAL RETREAT, April 17, 1956

Thirty of us arrived in time for supper last night to make the retreat with the Bishop. Cushioned chairs in the chapel — my first experience of this kind — radiant heated floors, most welcome on this cold, wet day, Formica on dining room tables — no table cloths — put the hot coffee pot directly on the table, running water in each room, no cupboard, simply four coat hangers, painted concrete block interiors, three quarter size beds. Not a penny wasted, completely adequate.

Jesuit retreat Master, of course. Makes no apologies — he is just a road marker. Whether the road marker is new and attractive, rusty and decrepit, it will get you there just the same. There were a few points about his talk I could argue about; his point in trying to establish the paganism of the times and country did not convince me. He did not convince me that I had to make a retreat to keep from deteriorating, For example — if a man wanted to destroy a house, all he had to do was leave it alone; if you did not cultivate a field, weeds would soon take over. But aren't we cultivating spiritually when we say daily Mass, rosary. Maybe he had a point but he was laboring the obvious. However, he sold me when he urged me to be generous, to be willing to go along, to make the best of this time of grace. He is a good sign post.

11:00

Just finished the morning's conference. It has been years since I felt like working at a retreat. For many, many retreats, I just let the retreat Master throw some ideas at me. But this morning, I read the account of the retreat in '37, in which I recorded that I made a Holy Hour morning and afternoon every day. So forthwith, I went off to the chapel and made a Holy Hour, mostly spent on the Way of the Cross. This one was for Dad; this afternoon it will be for Mother; tomorrow for Sis and uncle — and, of course, unto my own personal sanctification and through that channel unto the greater honor and glory of God.

This morning's conference sounded like it was routine stuff for laymen — the existence of God; the atheist's position (1%); the agnostics (21%); and the theists. At least 13 proofs from reason that God exists. Just one: Nothing can act until it exists. If there was nothing, there never could have been anything. Granted then existence of a first cause, that cause must have intelligence because nature is governed by laws, laws of astronomy, chemistry, botany. (It's the scientist's vocation to discover these laws.) But you could not have law if you did not have intelligence.

One gem, however, the retreat Master gave us, a new one to me: "Be as wise as serpents and as simple as doves," The serpent is the devil; be as smart as the devil. The dove is the homing pigeon. Release the homing pigeon anywhere and by means of an instinct we can't figure out, he makes a beeline for home. Conclusion: We belong to God.

9:00 p.m.

There is as much difference between my level of life and that of a blade of grass as there is between God's level and mine, and in order to participate in God's life, I must be in the state of grace, I must be free of mortal sin.

The fallen angels committed one sin and that was the sin of thought and thereupon God created hell. God, infinitely just, condemned these angels for eternity — the measure of the enormity of mortal sin,

April 18 — 10:00 a.m.

The retreat Master yesterday spoke quite frankly about mortal sin in a priest. Not the occasional mortal sin that sort of upsets a priest, but the contentment to remain in a mortal sin. He seemed to indicate that it is quite ordinary for a priest to be in the state of mortal sin from time to time during his life. He resented having been taken to task by a nun for having given a similar talk to nuns. The good Sister took the stand that mortal sin was quite foreign to religious.

No doubt the retreat Master is on the safe side — *tutior pars* — and, too, it may be proper to take such a stand during a retreat. I am of a generous nature, I don't think that Almighty God is so grievously offended by men of good will. I rather sympathize with the good Sister's attitude. A mortal sin is so enormous that it must counter-balance and over-balance all the good that the Sister or the priest has done.

It seems to me that the complacent priest, content to live in the state of mortal sin, is over-balancing all the good that he has done but the one who is "upset" by his deed, by that measure shows his eagerness to belong to God and such good will God will not reject, It was Archbishop Beekman who said at a day of recollection for priests: "Most Americans do not know how to go to hell."

I don't want to be smug; I want to be as far from mortal sin as east is from west. Neither do I want to make mortal sins when there are none, when penitents — clerical, religious or lay come to me for guidance. I don't believe that the priest who comes to confession to me every week, who wants to live the way God wants him to live, is in proximate danger of losing his soul. It is possible for him, by one deliberate act, to commit a mortal sin, like it is possible for him, deliberately and in full reflection, to tell the bishop to go to hell, or to rob a bank or to commit adultery.

I can't find it in me to be hard on the mother who has had six pregnancies in seven years (two miscarriages) and whose husband "has no self control." If she postpones her next pregnancy, she is not offending God as she would were she to commit adultery, as the wife would who refuses to have any children at all. I can't say to her that birth control is permitted; neither can I say to her that a deliberate venial sin is ever permitted, but I can say to her that I can't think God is going to send her to hell for what she had done.

It is no sin for me to take a high ball but I never heard of anyone taking a high ball for its nourishing quality. It is no sin for me to eat low calorie foods so that I can enjoy more eating. I know I am pointing to a dangerous parallel but I can't help pointing out that the two appetites God has given us are good; they are God's invention and I don't believe that the slightest perversion of either of these appetites offends Him grievously, I believe that a priest can offend God more by a Mass said carelessly, a Mass said with an eye for a stipend, than a wife who gives herself to her husband and under severe pressure frustrates conception.

Sunday, April 28, 1957 — 9:00 p.m.

About forty of us making the first clergy retreat to be conducted in our new retreat house, modeled, we are told this evening, after the Chicago retreat house. The retreat Master is a Jesuit,

He told us in his opening talk tonight that there are principally two conflicts in every priest's life. The first is the conflict between good and evil. Evil in a priest can be understood but never defended. The other is the conflict between the natural and supernatural, Priests deal in the super-natural; it's their profession, their business, The pull is to the natural away from the supernatural and it is not easy for a natural to do business in the supernatural field. It is very important that we reassure ourselves that to focus our attention on the supernatural. The retreat Master promised us to develop this theme.

Monday, April 29 — 11:15

A most remarkable retreat Master. Enough mental material in one talk to satisfy for the whole retreat; impossible to hold on to all of it.

If we look for material to complain about, we need not look far — it is always at hand. We can find mismanagement in the Church, always has been and always will be. But why go out of our way looking for it? The most common observation is: The Church must be divine to have survived its blunders, mistakes.

"Mirabiliter condidisti, mirabilior reformasti". Where do we go from here?

The evolutionist says that we are what we are by accident; our theology teaches us that we are what we are by design.

Whether we live a long life or not, whether we are healthy or infirm, if we are rich or poor, is immaterial,

5:00 p,m.

The dying priest sent for his confessor: the only thing I want is to save my soul; comfort, vacations, liquor, women. Priests as a class enjoy comfort, luxurious vacations, "one in sixteen" drinks too much. These things are all right in their place. But they must never be the end for which we live.

Tuesday, April 30, 1957 — 11:00 a.m.

The retreat Master speaks for forty minutes and never tires.

Today it was Christ the King. Everybody wants a leader. My desire is to follow Christ, to live like Him, to lead a life of mortification. This is the essence of my vocation. The running of the parish, doing good for others, is secondary.

Let's get back to our ideal as a seminarian. That seminarian was immature, green, perhaps not very intelligent, but he was on the level. He wasn't looking for a way to make a fast buck, he wasn't looking for a soft life, he wasn't going to ask anyone to do anything that he himself wouldn't be willing to do.

4:00 p.m.

Vice in a priest, alcoholism, sex, or lack of charity, is compensatory — the effect of a void brought on by a lack of prayer.

For some years now, I have simply been reciting a Pater, Ave and Gloria at each one of the Stations when making the Way of the Cross. I am going to go back to my old system. I am to make a classroom proposition out of it again. I am going to learn something, I'm going to meditate at each Station. And the lesson I learned at the XIII Station today, and the IV is to get closer to the Blessed Virgin by making more out of the rosary than getting the words in.

Thursday, May 2 — 8:30

I wish I could let myself go and put down what I would like. Though these pages are meant for no other eyes than mine, I am always conscious of the fact that someone some time may be snooping through these pages.

A retreat should not depend on the retreat Master. I am making this retreat and the truths expounded to me are not new. I find good in every retreat Master. This one, too, is solid, honest, sincere, interesting, firm, humorous. He told us on the second morning that some of the priests scandalized the Sisters by carrying conversations at breakfast on the first morning.

He asked for sacred silence at meals and after the evening meditation and, though the conduct of the group has been quite edifying, it is quite disturbing to have one or the other break the sacred silence. I notice that the retreat Master takes no recreations. Neither does Father Hillenmeyer, who is substituting for the Bishop.

We were told that we would not know whether we had made a good retreat until the end of the summer, perhaps not until Christmas.

We were told to make not more than one resolution. I have made one.

We had several times proposed for our edification the conduct of the laymen on retreat.

If we could choose between comfort and discomfort, between health and riches, between position and obscurity, between honor and being ignored — and receive the same eternal reward — which would we take? Which would, which did Our Lord take by preference? I have ordered a new car. Would I prefer to keep my old car? Would I choose ill health to well being? My health is excellent as of this moment, There was a time when I counted the hours of the retreat, the minutes of the talks. I am now under no pressure. I enjoy being good. Being good under pressure was a burden. Now that I am well, I can be very generous, now that I have everything: position, honor, income — it is easy to be generous but when I did not have it, was I just as generous or did I just give lip service, was I just kidding?

MARYDALE, April 14, 1958 — 9:00 p.m.

One day of our four day retreat is over. I have spent most of my time reading. Our retreat Master is a Passionist, dry but pithy; on regular confession, on attention in the recitation of the office, on sin, There is rarely such a thing as a single sin. Peter denied Christ three times, the accusers of Susanna lusted and then defamed and then were ready to be accessory to murder.

April 15

I have just finished reading "Atomic Apostle," a biography of Thomas Meyern, S.V.D. There is a lot I do not understand about this book. First, it was given to me and presumably to all pastors with the compliments of the S.V.D. Fathers. But the most puzzling thing about the biography is that there is no explanation of why a man who was a Vicar Apostolic in China should be assigned to Negro mission work in Mississippi. The pieces do not fit together.

While I write this, someone in a neighboring room has the opening ball game tuned in on his radio. How indifferent can we priests get concerning special times of grace! How scandalized we would be if a layman did a thing like that on the occasion of a retreat! Still, it is not for me to scold such a one. Out of the forty-four priests making this retreat, about forty are earnest about it but the few who are out of order make it appear that the whole body is colored with their brush,

I gave up in disgust yesterday because of the radio in the room next to mine, My neighbor even had his radio on after night prayers.

I find that I have to get up during the night to relieve myself. I find it is the ideal time to make my daily visit to the Blessed Sacrament. I got the idea one morning of the retreat and have tried it twice now and if I can do the same at home without disturbing anyone, I plan to continue this practice.

By way of making a firm resolution, I once more record my intention to discontinue smoking. This is by way of mortification because smoking does more harm than good. It is a matter of exercising will power. As someone pulls out a cigarette before me, I hunger for the first puff. If I thought of the fourth or fifth puff, I would pass up the cigarette. I, therefore, will begin on myself and proceed from there to be more positive in my direction to others.

Father Hanses and his consultors, including a young assistant, Father Lou Schmidt. Henry was way ahead of Vatican II in practicing collegiality.

MARYDALE, Monday, April 13, 1959 — a.m.

Father Gannon, S. J. is our retreat Master. His opening talk last night was on the question: WHAT DO I WANT OUT OF LIFE?

One man says money — another power — another wine, women and song. The unsophisticated child says — to know, love and serve God in this world and to be happy with Him in the next.

Father Gannon also pointed out that the real meditation begins when the formal talk is ended and the sine-qua-non of such a meditation is silence.

Whether we meditate along the lines outlined for us or along our own lines makes no difference, The particular thing I need is to deflate myself and see the good in others rather than seeing the faults in others rather than in myself. My priest penitents are a source of great edification to me — Fathers Fleming, Kamlage, Nieman, Steinhauser, Garvey, Hellmann. I never hear them belittling others in conversation, Sieg, Rosing all more generous in their outlook than the man they look to for direction. I'm going to look around during this retreat and focus my attention on those priests who are a source of edification to me. Emerson says that every man is my superior in some way. Every priest, I am sure, can edify me in some things, some priests in all things.

Tuesday, April 14th — 11:15 a.m.

Today I select Father Casey as my source of edification; Father Poole always, of course. I once served Father Mulhern's Mass and I note that he is just as reverential today as heretofore — not pompous, not individualistic. Today I am mindful of how Father Freiberg, God rest him, used to say the Domine non-sum-dignus.

I have been reading, just a wee bit, from Father Bruno Hagspiel's work "With the Silent Christ." It is a little overdone but it's just what the doctor ordered for me. More often than not, when I open my mouth, I put my foot in it, I'm going to do more listening.

Wednesday, April 15th — 2:30 p.m.

I just finished the Story of Thomas More by Farrow. What inheritance is mine! I never tire reading about More like I never tire reading Stevenson's defense of Damien. The particular lesson I would like to learn of More is the control of the tongue. Why must intelligent men, Christians, priests always find fault, belittle? My only safeguard is silence. When there are two or three gathered together, like or not, there is fault finding. Still it is not so — it is myself I am projecting. For my edifiers I shall select today Fathers Suedkamp and Hoppenjans and Hegenauer. Old Father Schmidt, on a cane.

silently smiling. Among the dead comes to mind, Father Coleman serving Mass all morning.

REMEMBER, NATURE SENT THEE HITHER BARE,

THE GIFTS OF FORTUNE, COUNT THEM BORROWED WARE.
Thomas˙More

Thursday, April 16th — 11:15 a.m.

Poor Father Haacke. After much hesitation, I include him among my edifiers. He is generous at Mass-serving, he is not hypocritical in his contacts during the day, he is in-and-out of the chapel all day — making the Way of the Cross, saying his rosary, But I can never trust him again. My conversations with him from now on will be common place generalities. He is not above quoting out of context for what reason he himself knows.

Fathers Ruschman, Whalen, Fischer — none of these sets the world on fire; they represent the vast majority of priests who live up to their ideal. When silence is sometimes broken, it sometimes seems that the whole body of retreatants are indifferent. When one analyzes the situation, one realizes that most of the retreatants are tending to business.

Thursday — 2:15 p.m,

For the record: somewhere I picked up the thought for reflecting at the second station. It's from Bishop Sheen — the greatest cross is to have no cross. It was the cross that made Thomas More, Abraham Lincoln what they were. At the sixth station — never did a woman let Christ down, where were the Apostles, the newly ordained priests? I just concluded conducting a retreat for twenty girls, members of the Baden Club of Cincinnati, at the Passionist's Monastery. Before beginning this retreat Sunday, I focused everything on this retreat to the girls around the Stations, principally the 2nd, 7th and 9th — sorrow for our sins of thought, word and deed. Word, sins of the tongue; deed, lack of mortification.

I have had Mary Ann Brinker very much in mind for the past month. When I call on her, I try to leave something special each time. For a coming visit, this thought from Abraham Lincoln: let's not ask the Blessed Virgin to get on our side, let's be sure we are on her side. Or again, our retreat Master told us of an old Jesuit brother who suffered constant severe pain. "How are you today, Brother?", he would be asked. And his answer: "Glory be to God, the pain couldn't be worse."

MARYDALE, May 3, 1960 — 8:00 a.m.

Father Tene Haynes, O.Carm. is our retreat Master. His opening conference last night said that a retreat was a matter of mind and will. At this moment, I am at the peak of my experiences. Everything that has gone before is now a part of my training and my faith, my priesthood should mean more to me now than ever before. And the will — we should not be saying our prayers like a child singing an adult love song, the meaning of whose words he does not understand.

Some time back, several priests were of the opinion that it would be more proper for a representative of the community to say Mass than for all of us to be crowding Masses in the basement chapel. I thought of that at my Mass this morning and I cast my vote for the practice. That is, I said Mass this morning *pro populo*. I made an act of reparation for the sins of the world, starting of course with my own. At the memento of the dead, I included in a special way all those who helped me to get where I am and lately I think more and more of uncle and I include them, also all the dead who had looked to me, depended on me for their spiritual welfare and my intention is, of course, to make up for any carelessness, deficiencies on my part. I do the same at the memento of the living — all those who helped me to get where I am by their prayers, by their support — financial, physical, moral — my housekeeper, janitor, Sisters, Assistant, members of the parish societies, contributors and all those who look to me to get them where they are going. This can be done at a community Mass but it is done more directly, intimately at an individual Mass.

May 3 — 11;15

There is one law that is above the law, the law of charity.

A chip carried too long can become a cross.

Luck is how you treat people,

May 4 — 7:45 a.m. — before breakfast

Again I said Mass pro populo, including all, living and dead who helped me to get where I am and are helping in the work of my priesthood.

Charity descends. I cannot give to those who have given to me except in desire, but I must pass on to those who come after me the inheritance that is mine.

The old live on in the past. I have seen misery and unhappiness but I have not experienced it. I have never heard an ill word about my father, I have none but grateful memories of my mother, my sister, uncle. Everything I have and am came to me from them and the Church, Father Beoletti, Father Bruno, Father Dyer.

MARYDALE, April, 1961 — Thursday

Father Arthur Meloche, a Canadian, is our retreat Master. His opening meditation was on the value of silence during retreat. I think it registered, though right now, I am disturbed by the mumbling going on next door. I think, too, that Bishop Ackerman's attitude toward his priests helps them in their priesthood. He is approachable, he has a fatherly interest in his priests, and yet he does not fraternize. I have never heard him praise the person of a priest, he does not attend the days of recollection, he does not show himself at clerical retreats. I am on my own. I am not observing the Bishop or wondering whether he is observing me.

Father Meloche covers too much ground in his talks, He holds our interest for almost an hour and has to be stopped by the clock. The thought I liked best — and have never heard brought out — to deal with impurity, be humble. Some priests make a fetish out of sex in dealing with the young; teach them humility. A measuring stick for humility is patience, Patience with bums, neurotics.

I died as a mineral and became a plant. I died as a plant and became an animal. I died as an animal and was a man, What should I fear? When was I less by dying?

Mahatma Gandhi.

Wednesday — 11:20

From the prayer to St. Joseph after Mass *"mente circontaminati, pura corda et caste corpore."*

A boy reaches his fulfillment when he become a father, a girl when she becomes a mother, Too many priests remain bachelors all their lives,

Wednesday — 8:15

The Blessed Virgin. His favorite statue of her shows her drying dishes. (St. Joseph on the other side rolls up his sleeves), She goes to Elizabeth to help. Zachary is no help — after all, he is a priest and dumb. At Cana, how does she know that there is no wine? She was out in the kitchen. By the way, how did they run out of wine? Our Lord's disciples had been invited and they were fishermen and men go fishing to do something besides catching fish. Passion Play in Toronto, Judas in desperation moans: What will I do, where will I go? A little girl in the audience calls out to him: "Go to Monimine!" That's the thing for us to do.

The last recorded words of Mary: Do whatever He tells you to do.

MARYDALE, Monday, April 22 — 8:00 p.m.

This retreat opened a half hour ago. Father Sprigler, Passionist, the first retreat Master that I recall who spoke without notes before him. His method is not to scold but to prod and he did it effectively. Am I going to go through this retreat or make it?

Most of the time in the past I just went through the retreat, just put in time. I look forward to retreat time as a time of rest, physical, mental, spiritual. This time I decided to make a retreat. I brought no secular reading matter. After all, the end of the line is closer than it has been and my chances are about one out of ten that I might wake up in eternity suddenly, judging by the number of our parishioners who die without a chance to make an act of contrition. And, after all, is the act of contrition more important than not sinning at all? It is not enough to merely plead "Lord, Lord."

10:00 p.m.

From the life of St. Vincent de Paul:

Their (Sisters of Charity) dignity lay not in their culture or social rank but in their being servants. . . . For this reason, authority never became command or demand: "Sister, would you like to do this for the love of our Lord?" An outsider would not have been able to tell the subject from the superior.

Tuesday — 11:50 a.m.

Very easy to listen to. At the end of forty-five minutes, I became conscious of the fact that I had not changed my position, had not crossed my legs. Faith, without it, it is impossible to please God. The theological virtue of faith is infused at Baptism. Before that, we were created according to the image and likeness of God, with intelligence and free will but by Baptism, we were infused with divinity.

Everything fits into God's plans. . . even our sins. St. Augustine. The Apostles — just ordained and then committed a sin that we could never match if we worked overtime at it. And only after that did our Lord say to them — Receive ye the Holy Ghost, whose sins you shall forgive, they are forgiven. Read Hebrews Chapter XI: (A pessimist is a fellow who, when he is given the choice between two evils, takes both of them,)

Afternoon

Sins of destiny — Alexander, Napoleon, DeGaulle, Reuther,

Evening

Sins of urgency — no circumquestrianism, horsing around,

Thursday — 8:45 a.m

Father Hillenmeyer, a priest for more than sixty years, is a source of constant edification to all who know him. He never breaks silence, even during recreation periods. Never puts on airs, never knocks. Lives in an old house, not interested in any luxuries. His only holiday is gardening and an occasional trip to his homestead, He could be drawing the limit in Social Security benefits but never applied, not interested. All priests to him are brothers, addressing us by our first name and we address him naturally as Father, not Monsignor, The richest man I know because he wants nothing but to serve in his vocation. Gets up with the Angelus in the morning, attends more functions like Forty Hours devotion than any other priest in the diocese, teaches in his school every day, never seems to tire. He was hard on one of his housekeepers whom I happen to know. If the tomatoes were ripe, she was told that they had to be canned that day — cleaning his room or washing and ironing and preparing complete meals was not important. He did not mean to be inconsiderate; he just figured that others could keep on going all day because it was so natural for him. Neither was he timid. If Bishop Mulloy took too much for granted, Father Hillenmeyer could stand his ground. But he never "pulled his rank" that I know of on those who worked for him. Father Hillenmeyer is the soul of the retreats I make with him.

MARYDALE, May 4 — 10:30 a.m.

Our retreat Master is an Augustinian, O.R.S.A. His opening conference last night made a parallel between Who is Christ? What think you of Him? And what is a priest? What do you think of him? And the first conference this morning was on pride — humility in the priesthood. So much honor, deference, confidence is shown a priest that he can very easily take unto himself a semblance of infallibility.

I have an appointment with Teresa Arens at the close of this retreat, who has had mental upsets. She is bringing a 24 year old girl friend who has turned to her for help, who also has mental upsets, who recently sat on the river bank until three in the morning. At first, she did not want to go to the priest with Teresa because all that the priest would tell her would be "to go to Communion every day."

I want to be the kind of priest that Teresa Arens thinks I am, or Loretta Langguth, or Alice Brinker, or Mrs. Rieheman, Roebker, Buckley, Felici or Charles, Bill, Gus, Doctor Weldon.

I want to be the kind of priest that Father Hillenmeyer is or Garvey, Deye, Hellmann, Hartman, the Brinkers, Sieg, Mueller and twenty, fifty others.

I am going to confession with that intention in mind. I'm going to clean the slate and aim again to be the kind of pastor that my clientele thinks I am.

Monday -5:45 p.m.

I have everything, why should I attempt to belittle others? Why should I emphasize the weaknesses of others? Why not habitually point out the good side of others? This struck me so forcefully during the last talk of the retreat Master, What purpose does it serve to pull others down. I believe that this is my outstanding weakness and as of this minute, the full force of this consideration could well be the principal fruit of this retreat.

When I speak of certain derogatory episodes in my relations with Bishop Howard or uncle, I am not even honest. I put the spotlight on some one particular event and take it out of its context. Do I intend to injure the estimation others have of such personages? Actually, I am proudly attempting to elevate myself by pulling the other fellow down. The easiest thing in the world is to find fault. Why not pity the other fellows weakness rather than expose it to ridicule.

MARYDALE, May 10, 1965 — 8:30 p.m.

Father Claude Leetham, a Rosminian from England, a Vatican Council theologian. He tells us that Father Rosmini, the founder of his order, had some of his writings on the Index because he strongly advocated the use of the vernacular in the Mass, that Church and State should be divorced and

Father Henry Hanses was mentor and friend to many a young priest, here shown with Father Tom Lubbers who died tragically April 29, 1975, in a motorcycle accident.

that the Church should dispossess itself of property before it is confiscated, However, he submitted to the authority of the Church.

He told us of the first chapter of the decree De Ecclesia. I missed much of the talk because of his brogue but I think he said that the Church never before defined itself and that now the Church is the union of all mankind under Christ — and service. I'll try to follow him better in succeeding talks. It looks like this retreat is going to be different, enlightening. Before last week, he never gave a clergy retreat in his life.

He took a sly dig at the many Monsignors present and because we have no canons in our diocese, he told a story about canons. Their catechism asks whether the office of canon was a sacrament. Yes, it is a sacrament; Of the living or the dead; no, it is not a sacrament of the living or the dead; it is a sacrament of the moribund.

MARYDALE, Tuesday, May 11, 1965 — 10:30 a.m.

No layman ever started a heresy. Canon Law does not mention the layman except to excommunicate him if he strikes the Pope, or sends his children to a public school. A new day is dawning. Now we must respect his liberty of conscience because of his intrinsic human nature. No longer is his function simply to pay. You give me your money, I'll build your school — where does not concern you and so on. No more,

Changes are brought about by someone breaking a rule. The changes in our liturgy were initiated by unauthorized people. People went to church because they committed a mortal sin if they did not go and you can't make them go along that way. The new liturgy, with emphasis on participation, will be attracting people to Mass.

The old argument that it was advantageous to have a uniform language all over the world was senseless. The poor don't travel. Only the well to do, priests and Bishops. Even so, the Eastern Rite doesn't use Latin.

Wednesday, May 12, 1965 — 10:45 a.m.

The retreat Master's brogue is so thick I can scarcely follow him. I got nothing out of last night's talk. This morning it was somewhat better, Divine Providence. I have been placed here and now for a definite purpose. He bordered on the fatalistic. Don't worry. You cannot by taking thought add a single cubit to your stature. Have confidence is all that it takes. A young man with initiative enters the seminary. There it is taken out of him. He becomes a priest and does not have it. Next comes frustration. Changing one's diocese does not help. Have confidence, make yourself available. God knows what is going on. One day, with nothing to do, he boarded a switch engine and told the engineer that God sent him to hear his confession, and for a half hour he rode along with him until the engineer finally loosened up. At the end of the run, he came across the engineer's boss. The boss asked him what he was doing in the cab. It ended up with the boss unburdening himself to the priest also. This is not so apt to happen on the golf course,

Wednesday — 12:05

The proper intention — before the job, on the job, after the job. The sins of the priest — cynicism, paralyzing the good efforts of others; self pity, the worst of all.

The pharisee — he bathed, he fasted, he went to church on Sunday. His sin was that he regarded himself better than the other fellow and he was, but the other fellow humbly said "Be merciful to me a sinner." The Good Samaritan, a Protestant, showed real charity.

Mortal, venial, deadly! A sin is a sin — that which offends Almighty God.

MARYDALE, May 24 — 9:15 a.m.

Father McCorry, S.J. is the retreat Master. I have been saying that the retreat Master is not important, the retreat's the thing. But Father McCorry does make you sit up and go along. His opening thought that a priest is a priest even in and especially in a secularized world. Whether the Church abolishes celibacy or priests give up their clerical garb, they are still priests. They are not primarily biologists or psychologists or editors but priests first and last. That was last night.

This morning I went to the chapel for my meditation. First comes faith and adoration and Lourdes always bolsters my faith. Then comes humility and contrition. And very forcibly today, for no apparent reason, it struck me that I never accuse myself in confession about pride, I am always comparing other priests' weaknesses with my strength. How much more wholesome it would be for me to compare their strength with my weaknesses. As of this moment, it seems to me that that consideration is going to be the principal fruit of this retreat.

Last year, the retreat Master listed among the sins of priests insidiousness. Though I often recall what he said, I find myself guilty of the very thing I was determined to practice. I find myself damning my confreres with faint praise, blowing up their idiosyncrasies instead of profiting by their example. My present resolution, to compare my weaknesses with the strength of others fits in with last year's resolution.

May 26 — 8:15 a.m.

The retreats I have made! Thirty of them recorded in this diary. Less and less application, more leisure, more comfort. Every room has a notice about silence, the napkins in the refectory inform us THAT ONLY IN SILENCE CAN WE SPEAK TO GOD. Not only do we have two recreations a day, but now we have conversation at meals and the day is ended by a free-for-all open discussion which goes on and on to break up in frivolity. If that is the way priests should make a retreat, why be so old-fashioned when lay folks make retreats.

No more office in common. Mass after breakfast, air-conditioned rooms, commode accommodations, fewer priests saying the rosary, making the Way of the Cross, going to confessions. And an alarming drop in vocations. And six inches from this diary is an ice-basket.

What's the answer? For me to tend my own corner of the wing and especially by example. One of the fruits of this retreat could be the good example that I give to others like that of Father Hillenmeyer, Goecke, Beiting, Wilson, Mulhern, McClanahan, Hartman, Modica, Merkle.

2:15 p.m.

Of all the good thought communicated to me during this retreat, I select that of the three P's as probably the best fruits, that which I can hold on to: PRAYER, PURITY AND PATIENCE. Again and again I have resolved to stop in the church on my way out or in to renew my good intention, I resolve to try again.

MARYDALE, May 16, 1967 — 9:15 a.m.

Father Whelan, Bostonian, Redemptorist is the retreat Master. Easy to listen to. Sincere, Practical. The man who has nothing puts on a front, the man who is something can easily be genuinely humble.

What odds will anyone give that we will all be together again next year? Forty-eight years ago this week, Ember Week, I was preparing for ordination on Ember Saturday. Alfred is five years older than I am and he is a very old man. Will I be as helpless five years from now? Now is the acceptable time, now is the time to face it, now is the time to reap the fruit of all of the spiritual seeds that I have sown in my life. Father Bioletti, Father Dyer, Elizabeth, mother, uncle, Ray Schmitz, Father Steinhauser, Father Deye, George Votel, Regie Tumler, Ann Johnson, Mary Agnes, Joe, Sisters Elizabeth Marie and Auxilia, Sister Grace, Father Sieg — these are the sermons — Edward Fedders — that have helped me most. Contemplate the beauty, the goodness of the past, revel in it, enjoy it, be grateful to Almighty God for His wonderful Goodness. I have had my heaven; to hold on to it, I must pass this legacy on to others and give to others what has been given to me. The hour is late.

Wednesday, May 18, 1967 -10:45

The retreat Master's ideas stream out like the bullet of a machine gun. Very difficult to summarize. Yesterday his theme was Faith, a supernatural gift that can be dimmed by not living in the presence of God, by placing things above Him. Today it was sin. Forget about the distinction between mortal and venial sin — sin is the rejection of God, the substitution of other things, like greed and sloth. Internal temptations can be more oppressive than external temptations. Turn these stones into bread; you don't get something for nothing. Throw yourself from the pinnacle; irresistible impulse.

MARYDALE, Tuesday, May 14, 1968 — 8:00 a.m.

Fifty years ago today, within the hour I was ordained sub-deacon. Daily I pray for those who helped me get to where I am (and for those who help me carry on in my vocation). I think of the little boy who fished from his father's shoulders, later to reflect that our best catches are often made from someone's shoulders.

I am what others have made me. Our family was always church centered. Uncle, a priest, two aunts in the convent. As an eight year old, I was sent to weekday Mass during vacation time. As a nine year, ten and eleven year old, I served Mass daily. As a six year old, a storm meant saying the rosary on my knees before a lighted candle. Then came St. Charles and Father Biveletti who put his arms around his boy penitents as they knelt beside him when confessing,

Skimming over the years, I come to Father Dyer. Always looked at the better side of people. "Trust every man once." "Never touch a woman." "Please tell the first one you meet that I turned you down."

Then St. John's Father Goebel — uncle loved me. Said once that he touched only two people in the world, Father Tappert and me. (To which I answered, how about the barber who shaves you?) His will, of long standing, turned all of his assets over to me, as did Father Alfred, who died since my last previous entry in this diary. Harry Hanneken, Clif Knapke, Joe Fedders — the girls who entered the convent — Josie Conrad, Catherine Suchanek. These are the folks who helped me get where I am. The College, the Latin School rounded out my education. Then came Himlerville where I prayed before the Twelfth Station; "I'll stick to it if it kills me," By today's standard, THOSE TWO YEARS WERE YEARS OF SACRIFICE, BUT LIFE WAS HARD FOR THE PARISHIONERS AS WELL AS ME; the mines closed, the bank failed, the floods washed the main street down the creek. That's when the boys went with me to the woods to eat and eat and eat beans and hot dogs I supplied. Then came Lynch, Angelo Meccia, John Dooley, the McCarthys, the Johnsons, the Carrolls, Dan Levello, Willie Raykovich, Miss Kaleman in Cumberland, the Trents and Krippenstaples in Harlan, Kathryn Overbeck and Ray and Margaret Cox.

This is some of my background. Sisters Elizabeth Marie and Auxilia were as generous as any of them. These are the people and the events that under God made me what I am. The Epistle of yesterday's Mass (Robert Bellarmine) spells out better than I can say what my life meant to me.

MARYDALE, Wednesday, May 15, 1968 — 8:45 a.m.

Got up after ten hours sleep; had breakfast, made the Way of the Cross out of doors for the dead I am indebted to, The first lecture is scheduled in a few minutes, then a concelebrated Mass at 10.:30. ARE WE ANY CLOSER TO GOD AS WE MAKE LIFE EASIER? Perhaps the best years of my life were the two spent in Himlerville where a quart of milk and an egg daily was included in my $15 a month rent — and the milk, the whole quart, I consumed for breakfast because I had no refrigerator. Like Martin Luther King, I had a dream. If the Bishop goes along with it, and if the plan will serve the diocese, I would like to retire to the Ida Spence Homes and live alone among the poor. I would gather some leaders around me; we would serve one another; I would drive sick people to the doctor. I would supply flowers, through the store, to beautify the lawn; I would provide garden seeds to high schoolers and garden space. I would not have air conditioning, no colored television; I would live on the same level with the people around me. I would give no money to anyone though I would hope to set up a St. Vincent de Paul Society. I would, however, pay well for work done for me. I would live alone like I did for nineteen years and I would never lock a door.

MARYDALE, Thursday, May 16 — 5:00 a.m.

I slept so well and long yesterday that I got up at 4:00 this morning and went outdoors. I sat on the porch listening to the patter of the rain. A lone plane glided silently by reminding me of the train whistle that I boarded one early morning while looking out the window of the washroom at Ellicott City. What is memory? By and by I went to the chapel. As I entered, a table lamp lit up. There was Paul Brinker. Had he been up all night? I said a Nunc-dimittis and meditated on some of the things the retreat Master had told us. What is memory? A train whistle of sixty years ago comes back to mind and what the retreat Master said yesterday does not seem so impressive now. We have security, we have the absolute truth, all the money in the world can't give us the best things in life; intellectual pleasure, spiritual comfort. We ruin it all when we measure our priesthood in dollars and cents.

Today, just today: not tomorrow, not yesterday, Tomorrow I say a Mass at Carmel Manor on the Anniversary of Father Nurre's Fiftieth Anniversary. Tomorrow evening, meeting of the diocesan senate. Saturday I say the funeral Mass for Msgr. Carroll in Covington. Sunday, I promised to go to Augusta for the closing of Forty Hours Devotion. Tuesday, I go to Lynch for the Golden Jubilee Celebration of the parish. On Decoration Day, we will have an outdoor Mass at our Cemetery; on June 1, the parish picnic; on June 2nd, confirmation at the Cathedral for our converts. Today. Just today. The end of the retreat, followed by Fr. Streck's Golden Jubilee celebration.

MARYDALE, May 6, 1969 — 9:15 a.m.

The beauty of the psalms struck me this morning like rarely before. In today's office, there is nothing, so far, about preparing my arm for war, make of my foe's wife a widow, his children orphans. Oh, Lord in your anger, punish me not . . . Oh Lord, all my desire is before you, from you my groaning is not hid . . . Neither in my youth, nor now that I am old, have I seen a just man forsaken. Psalm 36. Be not vexed over evil doers, nor jealous of those who do wrong. . . The Lord watches over the lives of the wholehearted, their inheritance lasts forever.

What misery I have been spared! A good home, Sulpician training, generous support all my life, (Except Bishop Howard who supplied the deflation that kept me humble.) Another priest had similar background, but he was timid and I suppose when a certain lady gave him a crutch to lean on, he surrendered and seeks now his support from a human being rather than his Creator. Tuesday's psalms. I hope some day to be his crutch.

MARYDALE, May 7, 1969 — 9:30 a.m.

I made the Way of the Cross last night in the dark along the lake shore. The Twelfth Station always reminds me of Himlerville, where I prayed at this Station: I'm going to stick to it even if it kills me.

My days at Himlerville contributed immensely to my priestly formation, I have no cross to bear today but when one has no big troubles, he makes big ones out of little ones. I find myself making crosses out of nothing — Sister Rosina, Father Hilz, like the assistants before him. With the Twelfth Station in mind, I hope to make stepping stones out of little crosses that come my way.

MARYDALE, May 8th — 9:15 a.m.

Our retreat Master is Bishop Bernadine, a humble, sincere priest. Who is the priest's pastor? Each one of us. I was asked to attend a meeting of nine priests after the last conference to see if we could do something to increase fraternal charity among us priests.

Monsignor Henry Hanses. He had to pose for this one.

May 19th is the Anniversary of Bishop Ackerman's installation as Bishop of Covington. It was decided to begin with the Bishop and will take a full page ad in the Messenger ($110) to tell the diocese that the priests revere and respect our Bishop. Next, three or four ordinandi are from outside the Diocese. We will individually do all that we can to make them feel at home with us. And, finally, we agreed to spend a half hour a week in prayer for one another. I will reserve my Saturday's preparation for Mass for this intention.

MARYDALE, May 26, 1970 — 11:00 a.m.

The retreat Master is a "pinch hitter," a substitute, a French Canadian, eleven years a priest. Very forceful. I know of no priest ten years or twenty years ordained who can speak with such authority. Everything up to now belongs to the past. Always true but especially since man stepped on the moon. But the community of Saints goes on — we must not be afraid to risk,

Shall I risk? If I consulted my own desires, I would like to retire to live the life of a poor man. We hear more and more of inner-city apostolates, of a need to identify with the poor, Catholics, local, are going up the economy ladder, the poor are being left further behind, more of them non-Catholics. Priests identify themselves more and more with the affluent: professional income, air conditioned car, luxurious vacations. Sisters, too, move into apartments, socialize, wear modern dress — and vocations decrease.

Have I the courage to retire and take up my residence in a government housing? Nothing would suit me better but will the Bishop approve? And what do I leave behind me? Henry Krumpelman, Esther Saalfeld, the whole team that works with me at St. John's. Some day there will be another pastor at St. John's and he will build up his own team. I have only a few years of activity left. I would like to live among the poor, take them to the doctor, help them get their food stamps, build up their self-respect. And let another priest, in his prime, take over at St. John's.

RISK? I am not afraid of it. I dread looking forward to retirement at Carmel Manor or as a Sister's chaplain in a spoiled child environment. I will have to decide soon, before I become incapacitated, Only five priests are still active: Towell, Streck, Carlin, Merkle and Deimling, The Priest's Council would like to see an age deadline. Only Bishop Ackerman is holding on to everything he has. Right now, I must decide to confide in the Bishop. I think he wants me to carry on but is it fair to priests who long for our position of responsibility? Father Deye has been appointed a pastor at 59. Men in their forties and in their thirties could do my work at St. John's at least as effectively as I am doing. And the poor need a friend, too! I am waiting for the psychological moment. It takes courage to take risks at 73.

May 27th — 7:15 a.m.

We say Mass at 5:30 p.m. concelebrated very satisfying, I awoke at 6:30, took a walk while meditating and here I am, reinforced in my wish to retire, I told my story to Father Finn yesterday and he reassured me, The retreat Master then gave a talk in which he said that the Cardinal of Canada, who resigned his see to work among the lepers, had suffered a crisis of faith. That makes sense to me. This morning I read an article on the Spectre of Cultural Imperialism. In hunger stricken Brazil, one can buy a Barbie Doll, together with a guide book on the clothes she will need to keep well dressed. "No colonial system can function without a Herodian class, a dependable cadre of native quislings who will carry out empire's will in the province"...The power that holds them is the media- purveyed beatific vision of a consumer paradise: T.V. sports car, transistor and Barbie Dolls... And the U. S. controls the means of grace.

Consumer paradise, that's what ruined Adam and Eve. I want to live the life of a poor man because I am convinced that that will strengthen my faith. That's my heritage. My parents came from a village whose people were measured by the size of the manure pile next to their door. Father Goebel had it "made" but his greatest luxury was his pipe and his Epicurean delight with pumpernickel.

I am drafting a letter to the Bishop today, I am not asking for something. I am saying that if he thinks it is in the best interest of religion, I would like to begin an apostolate among the poor. Since I committed myself to the priesthood, this is the first time that I have channeled my work. I find it harder and harder to make decisions. The retreat may mark a turning point in my life.

May 28th — 11:00 a.m.

I have made a draft of a letter. I will type and send it to the Bishop tomorrow. I have made my decision. The rest is up to the Bishop,

This morning, Father Streck asked Father Mielech to take him to Dr. Dornhagen. I think the days of Father Streck's service to the Church are coming to an end. Father Towell has to be assisted when he rises from a deep chair. Father Deimling is also my senior by a year or two. I just went to confession to him and he is very much confused by the communal commitment that the retreat Master is asking us to make. I tried to explain it to him but it was beyond him. That leaves Father Merkle and Father Carlin, the last two that are seniors to me and are still in service. Father Merkle is quite stooped but I think still in complete possession of his faculties. Rumor has it that Father Carlin is about to retire. Father Danz, a junior to me, is about to retire. Fortunately, we have six newly ordained men this year but only one coming up next year and the prospects beyond that are dim. What would I do if I were the Bishop and a priest like me asked for retirement? Rumor also has it that Bishop Ackerman was to have said that we will keep the seminary going another year. That would release a half dozen priests — Father Smith, the vice-rector, has just been given a parish, Father Deye has been appointed pastor of Corpus Christi. Is the faculty being fazed out? The Louisville Seminary is closing and has advertised in the Wall Street Journal that its property is for sale.

MARYDALE, Tuesday, May 11 — 10:45 a.m.

Retreats are falling off — more and more priests are making private retreats. For my part, I look forward to these days, as much as a vacation as a spiritual retreat. Father Hillenmeyer is here and he is always an outstanding model to the rest of us,

I have been saying that 95% of a priest's retreat is atmosphere. But this year's retreat Master is dynamic, whatever that means. It reminds me of dynamite. He shocked me at first by appearing before us in the chapel in shirt sleeves, and then he explained that his habit — he is a Norbertine — was lost somewhere between here and there.

His talk this morning was on charity but the English language is bankrupt when it comes to expressing abstract notions. Love means kindness. First to our brothers who are leaving the priesthood — and so on down the line until he got to the traffic cop about whom he wrote to his boss. It was the first time that someone has said something nice about his cop and the boss had the letter laminated and hung on the wall.

Thursday — 1:00 p.m.

We are asked to evaluate our retreat.

Permissiveness leads to laxity (only one priest out of four in Detroit makes a retreat). Retreats should be made compulsory; private retreats should be by way of exception. My commitment was made to God; not to the Church.

MARYDALE, June 7 — 3:00 p.m.

Last January I thought I would die, I asked for another chance — my prayer was heard. But my prayer was not an act of contrition but an act of thanksgiving. If I were to spend my life on my back, I would never get back to thank God for what He has done for me.

I don't know how long I will live, maybe a year, a month, or a week.

God could not have blessed me more than He did. I love everybody, my crosses were stepping stones, even my sins. My dad, my mother, my brother, my sister, uncle, here I am.

MARYDALE, August 1973

TO FOOL OTHERS — VENIAL SIN.

TO FOOL OURSELVES — MORTAL SIN.

WE MANUFACTURE DEGREES.

WE DO NOT MANUFACTURE MORALITY.

TEMPTATION — A SIGN TEMPTED.

SERMONS MUST BE ELOQUENT.

EXAMPLE MUST BE MORE ELOQUENT.

MARYDALE, June 1975 — 4:30 am.

My last entry in my diary. GRATITUDE! The little boy who fished from his father's shoulder. Father Dyer, 60 years ago, always looked on the brighter side of other people. The examples of Sisters Elizabeth and Auxilia, Sisters Andre and Grace, Father Bioletti, uncle, Streck — who didn't know an unkind word about the devil.

GRATITUDE! The sacrifices made by my mother, father, sister, uncle, by Himlerville, Mrs. Kelemens.

GRATITUDE! To God, my Father, who blessed me more than I deserved.

MARYDALE, May 1976 — 4:30 am.

MY FINEST HOUR.

In 1926, Bishop Howard sent me to the Big Sandy.

I arrived in the coal camp of Himlerville in Martin County via West Virginia on the mail passenger coach next to the driver. Eventually I rented two rooms for $15.00 a month, utilities included, besides an egg and quart of milk every day while in town. I did not have an ice box,

I am told not to make any appeal in the name of the missions. My first annual report to the diocese showed $9.00 on hand. The report came back because I did not include $45.00 cathedraticum.

I asked Bishop Howard for help. I got one sentence reply: "I will not be able to grant your request." My Bishop said to me: "I tried to make a teacher out of you and I knew that you would not make a missioner."

I knelt before the 12th Station and prayed: I will stick to it if it kills me. I canceled my subscription to America and the Ave Magazine, though America ignored my request.

Father Hanses spent his last days at Carmel Manor. Even then, as the photo shows, he was people-centerd.

I wanted to get a spiritual reading book but I could not afford to charge it. A year later, the Daughters of Isabella asked Bishop Howard for a mission project and he assigned to them the Himlerville mission. I got $400.00.

In 1928, the mine in Himlerville went bankrupt and a flood wiped out the main section of the town. Himlerville became a ghost town.

With a heavy heart, I left Martin County, Traveling through West Virginia and Virginia, I arrived on the Trail of the Lonesome Pine, in the rain, at night, at my new assignment, Harlan County.

Now I am retired at Carmel Manor, Joseph Kennedy with all his millions could not get better care than I get here. My financial problem now is how to dispose of my money. I told Bishop Ackerman that I did not want his monthly check. (I am now on Uncle Sam's payroll.) He said: "Do whatever you want with it."

After more than 50 years in the priesthood, my finest hour was when I knelt before the 12th Station in Himlerville. Bishop Howard was a heavenly instrument to teach me discipline. *"Crux mihi dux"* was the motto of the Bishop who ordained me, Bishop Maes.

MARYDALE, May 10, 1977 — 10:15 a.m.

Father Louis Brinker came to confession last night. I told him that this retreat may be my last. For several years I have thought each retreat would be my last. Atmosphere is the whole thing. Father Hillenmeyer was my model, he was the retreat. I am the oldest. Am I a model?

FROM MARYKNOLL, May 1977

IN A LITTLE POOL
I WONDER: HOW
SHOULD ONE RIGHTLY MEASURE!
BY THE EARTH THAT HOLDS IT?
BY THE HEAVENS IT HOLDS?
MY LIFE? HOW MEASURE IT?
BY HEALTH, BRAIN, SEX, POSSESSIONS -
OR BY THE HEAVEN IT REFLECTS?

Epilogue

June 14, 1969 — 50th Anniversary of Ordination

We are gathered here this morning to offer up the sacrifice of the Mass. What we are doing here, we believe, has the same efficacy as the sacrifice offered up at the Last Supper, the same efficacy as the sacrifice on the Cross. From the rising of the sun to the going down therefore a clean oblation is offered up to Almighty God all over the world, in atonement for man's sin and to satisfy God's justice.

By the plan of Divine Providence I have been privileged now for fifty years to be one of Our Lord's agents, to be a ladder between man and God and that thought should make any sane man humble. For fifty years I, like my brother priests, have been praying, first, for all present; secondly, for all Christians, living and dead. To this, I have from the very beginning added a general intention of my own. I pray first for all those who helped me get to where I am; secondly, for all those who help me in my apostolate, and third, for those who count on me to be a channel of God's grace for their spiritual welfare and by this means I hope to make up for the failures that I have been guilty of.

It is generous of you to pray with me on this special occasion and I humbly ask you to join your prayers to mine, as I will join my prayers to yours, in the hope that we will all right merrily bask in the sunshine of God's smile throughout eternity!

REVEREND MONSIGNOR HENRY A. HANSES

<u>Born</u>: October 28, 1896, Detroit, Michigan — St. Boniface Parish

<u>Parents</u>: Henry Hanses and Baldwina Goebel

<u>Education</u>:
        Elementary — St. Boniface, Detroit, Michigan
                St. Augustine, Augusta, Kentucky
        Secondary — St. Charles, Ellicot City and Catonsville, Maryland
        College— St. Charles, Ellicot City and Catonsville, Maryland
        Philosophy — St. Mary Seminary, Baltimore, Maryland
        Theology — St. Mary Seminary, Baltimore, Maryland

Scenes from the party celebrating Father Hanses being named a Monsignor. Smiles were rampant! (Ray Hadorn photos)

Ordained: June 14, 1919, Covington, Kentucky by Most Rev. Ferdinand Brossart, at Cathedral Basilica of the Assumption

Assignments:

1919 — Covington, KY, St. John Church, Assistant Pastor

1920 — Covington, KY, Mother of God Church, Assistant Pastor

1921 — Mountain Missions (St. Casimir, Van Lear; St. Stephen, Himlerville; Resurrection, Lynch), Pastor

1945 — Covington, KY, St. John Church, Assistant Pastor

1954 — Covington, KY, St. John Church, Pastor

1971 — Resigned as Pastor, St. John Church, Covington, KY
Became Associate Pastor, St. John Church, Covington, KY

1975 — Retired, Residence at Carmel Manor, Ft. Thomas, KY

Domestic Prelate: — August 30, 1950; Invested, April 22, 1954

Died: Tuesday, January 19, 1982, St. Luke Hospital, Ft. Thomas, KY age 85, ordained 62 years.

Interment: St. John Cemetery, Ft. Mitchell, KY

Homily given by Rev. Anthony Deye, January 22, 1982 at the funeral of Father Henry Hanses

Bishop Hughes, Bishop Ackerman, Relatives of Father Hanses, Brothers and Sisters in Christ:

These reflections on the virtue of love, or charity, are intended to focus your attention on the sermon which Father Hanses preached in action over the past 85 years.

Charity, or love, of course, is of the essence of Christianity. The primacy of love is emphasized by Christ when he sums up the entire law in the twofold command of love of God and love of neighbor (Luke X, 27-28). St. Paul in his letter to the Corinthians (I Cor. XIII, 4-7) describes it in these words: "Love is patient and kind; love is not jealous or boastful; it is not arrogant or rude. Love does not insist on its own way; it is not irritable or resentful; it does not rejoice at wrong, but rejoices in the right. Love bears all things, believes all things, hopes all things, endures all things." And he concludes with the words: "So faith, hope, love abide, these three; but the greatest of these is love."

This love should be universal. When asked: "Who is my neighbor?" Christ explained its universality with the story of the Good Samaritan, charitable help from a stranger. Yes, we are asked to forgive our enemies and to do good to those who hate us.

This love must be practical. It must show itself in deed and not just be expressed in words. St. James writes (James II, 14-17): "What does it profit, my brethren, if a man says he has faith but has not works? Can his faith save him? If a brother or sister is ill-clad and in lack of daily food and one of you says to them, "Go in peace, be warmed and filled", without giving them the things needed for the body, what does it profit? So faith by itself, if it has no works is dead."

Countless men and women, by their heroic lives, have illustrated the Christian message, as apostles, martyrs, intellectuals, penitentials, etc. But of all the saints there is one who has won the special universal admiration of both Christians and Non-Christians -St. Francis of Assissi. He did so by practicing charity in a spirit of humility, simplicity, and poverty. There is no way of measuring his impact on society, but no one could deny that it has been great.

It's natural to think of Father Hanses as a reflection of St. Francis. Many of you can recall stories illustrating the confidence Father Hanses placed in people, his willingness to help everyone, and at all costs. It wasn't as if Father Hanses were naive about finance or human behavior. He was an intelligent businessman and an objective appraiser of human beings. It was simply that in helping people he was willing to bet on human beings even when he knew the odds were against him.

Father Hanses spent practically the first half of his priestly life, 1921-1945, serving the people in the Kentucky Mountains, especially in the Lynch-Cumberland-Harlan area. Natives and immigrants, the latter especially from southern and eastern Europe, found in Father a gentle guiding and helping hand. Through his help, Catholic young people found their way to Catholic academies and Villa Madonna (now Thomas More) College.

Even today, apostolic work in Appalachia demands more than the average in physical and social sacrifice. Many of us might have found work in Appalachia in the 1920's difficult and isolated, when autos were primitive, highways non-existent, and priests few and scattered. To this, one could add the depressed economic conditions of the 1930's. But Father Hanses was at home in the Mountains and happy because he loved the people and identified with them, Catholics and Non-Catholics, natives and immigrants. The Mountain area was his home.

This same commitment he showed in the inner-city of Covington in the second half of his priestly life, in pastoral work at St. John's Church, 1945-1975.

We mentioned earlier that charity, or love, should be universal. Father loved everyone and opened his door to everyone. First of all were his parishioners, his beloved people of St. John's, whom he knew, loved and served. There were also the priests, religious, and lay people from outside the parish, who wore a path to his door. He was involved in interracial work, labor relations, ecumenism, civic affairs, the creation of a credit union, fostering the St. Vincent de Paul Society, organizing and serving on the Priests' Senate, teaching and counseling at Villa Madonna (now Thomas More) College, etc.

As St. James wrote, charity must show itself in action. Father Hanses was not a mere theorist or speaker. He solved problems. If a black family needed a home, he just happened to have one he could rent to them. If someone needed money, he came up with it. If someone needed a job, he found one. With Father Hanses, there was no such thing as a problem that could not be solved. Even in retirement, he continued to help at St. John's and was a source of strength to those who came to him and a source of edification to all at Carmel Manor.

Both individually and collectively, we will miss Father Hanses. Hopefully, his life will stand before us — priests, religious, laity, Catholic and Non-Catholic, young and old — as a beacon of light.

In closing, I would change the familiar Franciscan prayer into a statement of fact:

Lord, you made him an instrument
of Your Peace.
Where there was hatred,
he sowed love.
Where there was injury, pardon
Where there was doubt, faith
Where there was despair, hope
Where there was darkness, light
Where there was sadness, joy
He sought not so much to be
consoled as to console
To be understood as to understand
To be loved as to love.
May he rest in peace.

The world lost a great humanitarian, priest and saintly man when Henry was called home.

WANTED

Old Photos • Letters • Articles
Stories • Anecdotes • Diary Accounts

Names, Addresses and Phone
Numbers of Living Friends

Names of Deceased Close Friends
and Their Spokespersons
to Contact

All Dedicated to Producing A Biography Of

FATHER HENRY HANSES (+Jan. 19, 1992)

Of The Covington Diocese

All borrowed materials will be returned

Write: The Henry Hanses Project
c/o St. Henry Church
3813 Dixie Highway
Erlanger, KY 41018
Or Phone: (606) 727-2105

An enlargement of an ad that invited people to send in their stories and memorabilia of Henry Hanses. The office is still open.

New book tells stories of Father Henry Hanses

Diane Reder
Staff Writer

In 1921, a young priest, only 25 years old, from the Covington diocese went to serve the mountain people of Eastern Kentucky. His ministry there lasted for 24 years.

"Ask anyone who knew Father Henry Hanses and you're likely to hear, 'He was a saint!'" wrote Father Ralph Hartman, a retired priest of the diocese, in the prologue of a new book, "Fr. Henry Hanses —How Handsome Before the Lord".

The book, which was prepared and edited by Father Hartman, is actually the diary kept by Father Hanses beginning Aug. 28, 1926 and ending May 10, 1977.

Father Hanses served the Harlan County area of Eastern Kentucky including Lynch, Van Lear, and Himlerville. His diary describes his travels from one area to the other, frequently by foot as he had no car or horse.

His notes from Oct. 25, 1926 give an idea of what his ministry was like: "Either Wednesday or Thursday I am going to Wayland; the next day to Estill; then by horse to Ligon, train to Wheelwright on the same day; that night Weeksbury for Sunday. Monday morning, All Saints' Day, I plan to leave Weekbury at 4 a.m. and will get to Louisa at 10 a.m. for Mass there; then by bus to Ashland, stopping long enough to hear the Sisters' confessions, Tuesday morning, if I can't make it Monday night."

"His generosity was so widely known that people lined up to get help, but they also lined up to give him things as well," recalls Msgr. John Murphy in the prologue of the book. Father Murphy recounts the time that he went to Father Hanses to borrow $2,000 to give to a former student who was having hard times.

"Henry quickly gave me the money for him and, later, when I was worried that it hadn't been paid back, he told me not to worry and that when it was paid back, I should keep it and lend it to someone else who might need it," Father Murphy said.

and Father Hanses became pastor of the parish.

"He always impressed me as a very original person. His philosophy, his whole response to the challenge of ministry of the priesthood and the call of God in his life seemed so fresh and vital," said Father Hartman who first met Father Hanses when he was pastor at St. John Parish.

"He was a very admirable person albeit a little bit extraordinary because he often challenged the status quo," Father Hartman said. "He was a great problem solver. He learned early in life not to take no for an answer. He was one of those people who fully believed that, with God's help, there was a third solution to a dead-locked problem."

Father Hartman said that the book would not have been possible without the financial support of Father Hanses' good friend, Katherine Landwehr, who wanted to see the diary published. She first met Father Hanses after World War II when she was trying to find food and clothing to send to the needy people in Europe. She was not a member of St. John Parish, but Father Hanses helped her with this project.

"Father Hanses was a man of God who gave his life to help the people of God," she said. "He was a tremendous person. He fed every hungry person that came to his door. He would give them a ticket for a nearby restaurant. One month the bill equaled his salary.

"He is an example to the young people of this diocese, particularly, to see the need that Christ has for their labor and how in the end it can make a saint out of them."

"Whether we have a sell-out, or break even, or lose money is not the highest concern to Katherine," Father Hartman said. "She wanted to see the diary circulated. She hopes it will find its way into seminary libraries and places where young men preparing for the priesthood might have Henry offered to them as a role model."

Father Hanses retired as pastor of St. John Parish in 1971 after having a stroke. He died in 1982. The book is available for purchase at Mother of God Church, St. John Church, and the *Messenger*.

The diaries of Father Henry Hanses have been combined in book form by Father Ralph Hartman as a tribute to Father Hanses, who was one of those people who "fully believed that, with God's help, there was a third solution to a dead-locked problem," according to Father Hartman.

Saint Henry Church

3813 DIXIE HIGHWAY
ERLANGER, KENTUCKY 41018
(606) 727-2035

May 24, 1999

To the Bishops and Seminary Rectors
of the United States:

Greetings in the Name of the Lord,

I am happy to enclose a complimentary copy of a brief diary of Father Henry Hanses, a priest of the diocese of Covington. On the reverse side is an article about this publication from The Messenger, the diocesan newspaper.

Those who knew this remarkable priest believe that his life and spirit have something to say to young man today who may consider becoming priests. This is the conviction of Katherine Landwehr who funded this project, a local woman who would like to see every seminarian read this story of faith.

I hope you will enjoy the book and pass it on to others seeking to know the Lord in the life of a great priest.

Sincerely,

Rev. Ralph C. Hartman
retired

(606) 581-7719